The
polysecure
WORKBOOK

The
polysecure
WORKBOOK

Healing Your Attachment and Creating
Security in Loving Relationships

Jessica Fern

 THORNAPPLE PRESS

The Polysecure Workbook
Healing Your Attachment and Creating Security in Loving Relationships

Thornapple Press
300 – 722 Cormorant Street
Victoria, BC V8W 1P8
Canada
press@thornapplepress.com

Thornapple Press is a brand of Talk Science to Me Communications Inc. and the successor to Thorntree Press. Our business offices are located in the traditional, ancestral and unceded territories of the ləkʷəŋən and W̱SÁNEĆ peoples.

Cover design by Brianna Harden
Interior design by Jeff Werner
Editing by Andrea Zanin
Proofreading by Alison Whyte

Library and Archives Canada Cataloguing in Publication

Title: The polysecure workbook : healing your attachment and
    creating security in loving relationships / Jessica Fern.
Names: Fern, Jessica, author.
Identifiers:
    Canadiana (print) 20220286345 | Canadiana (ebook) 20220286361 |
    ISBN 9781990869044 (softcover) | ISBN 9781990869051 (EPUB)
Subjects:
    LCSH: Non-monogamous relationships—Psychological aspects. | LCSH:
    Non-monogamous relationships—Psychological aspects—Problems,
    exercises, etc. | LCSH: Attachment behavior. | LCSH: Attachment
    behavior—Problems, exercises, etc. | LCGFT: Problems and exercises.
Classification: LCC HQ980 .F47 2022 | DDC 306.84/23—dc23

Digital print edition 1.0

CONTENTS

INTRODUCTION

Welcome to *The Polysecure Workbook!*

After the publication of *Polysecure: Attachment Trauma and Consensual Nonmonogamy* in October 2020, I quickly received many requests for a workbook to go along with the book. Readers generally loved *Polysecure* and adamantly expressed wanting to go even deeper in creating a more secure *attachment* within themselves, with their partners or both. Although people have become increasingly aware of individual attachment styles and the need for relationship safety and security in the last decade, the steps people can take to get there have not always been clear. This is especially true for people practicing non-monogamy, who have typically been excluded from the mainstream literature on the concept of attachment, or when included, they are misunderstood, misrepresented and even pathologized. *Polysecure* was the first book to apply attachment theory to nonmonogamous relationship structures. In it, I encourage nonmonogamous readers, making it clear that you can have multiple secure attachments and you don't have to act in strictly monogamous or hierarchical ways to get there. *Polysecure* also emphasizes the utmost importance of creating a more secure attachment with yourself, regardless of your relationship orientation or style.

This workbook is meant to be a companion guide to accompany you on your *polysecure* journey. Like *Polysecure*, this workbook is divided into three parts. In Part One you will focus on your own attachment history with your childhood attachment figures, your resulting attachment styles as an adult, your different attachment experiences on the multiple dimensions of the nested model of attachment and trauma, and how to find more acceptance of your past and release ways of thinking that no longer serve you. In Part Two you will explore your *why* for practicing nonmonogamy, the different styles of nonmonogamy that you relate to, your experiences of relying on relationship structure for your attachment security, and the specific ways that you may have experienced attachment challenges, changes and ruptures throughout your process of becoming and being nonmonogamous. Part Three attends to the *safe haven* and *secure base* foundations of being polysecure and discusses how to apply HEARTS in your relationship with partners and yourself. (HEARTS is an acronym for a concept I wrote about in *Polysecure* that articulates six specific things you can do to cultivate secure attachment in your multiple relationships.) Part Three ends with walking you through some contemplations and ideas for assessing your level of polysaturation and how to create your own temporary vessel where you stage which *consensual nonmonogamy* (CNM) activities you will initially begin with and which ones you will add in later, down the road, to best support a sustainable pacing when there are attachment struggles at play.

In each chapter, you'll find a summary of the concepts and ideas of the equivalent chapter in *Polysecure*, with new additional questions, prompts and exercises designed to support you in your further exploration and integration of the material. This workbook is intended for people who are already acquainted with *Polysecure*. If you haven't read *Polysecure*, I do invite you to read the book since it provides the concepts and theories that lay the foundation for the exercises that you will explore in this workbook. However, I also know that everyone learns and grows differently, and some people prefer to jump straight into the practice with little of the theory. That approach can work here, too.

You can go through this workbook by yourself or with your partners, friends, loved ones, a therapist or a group. I suggest setting aside regular times to move through each section and chapter of the workbook. Go at your own pace. As I often say to people making the transition from monogamy to nonmonogamy, this process is a marathon, not a sprint, and this is also entirely true for the process of healing our insecure attachment. Bringing your commitment, persistence and patience on this healing expedition will serve you well. Processing your past and creating a coherent narrative of what you went through and how it impacted you is an important part of building an earned secure attachment style, so that you can live more fully in the present with yourself and your partners. Step by step, you will create a more secure attachment with yourself. Furthermore, gaining more clarity about who you are, what you want and what you need will undoubtedly support you in your adult attachment-based relationships. This workbook will help illuminate the hardships you went through for the purpose of creating new personal and relational freedoms.

Some of the questions and exercises might feel easy and straightforward; others might be challenging and bring up grief about the hardships you went through and the love, *attunement* or protection that you didn't receive. As you go through the different activities and prompts, it is normal to experience a mix of insight, relief, anger, overwhelm, fear, a sense of renewal and needed release. Please make the space to allow all these different feelings to be present. Holding an attitude of curiosity and courage is important here. It takes tremendous bravery to confront childhood trauma and attachment ruptures. You are not broken and in need of fixing. Rather, you are in need of care and nurturance for the unique attachment experiences you went through. Trauma can be experienced on a spectrum from the more extreme to the more subtle or even socially acceptable. Every person will have different wounds from what they've faced, regardless of where their experiences fall on that spectrum.

You are on a path of restoring your relationship with yourself and also possibly with your partners. In its essence, this is walking the path of love for self, for others and for the world. With that said, this workbook is not meant to replace professional or medical treatment. Instead, it is meant to be one of the supportive companions for your healing and growth. I am truly excited for what lies ahead of you with this workbook and I am deeply grateful to further accompany you on your polysecure journey.

Part *One*

CHAPTER ONE

OVERVIEW OF ATTACHMENT THEORY

Summary

Healthy attachment is a deep bond and an enduring emotional closeness that connects people to one another across space and time. As human infants, we are born into this world with an attachment system that wires us to expect connection with others. John Bowlby called this innate expectation the attachment behavioral system and explained that it's one of several behavioral systems that humans evolved to ensure our survival. As infants, we can't yet meet any of our own needs. So, in order to survive, we have to bond and attach to care-takers who can provide us with food and shelter as well as meeting our biological and psychological needs for emotional attunement, warm responsiveness and calming physical touch.

When an infant feels fear, distress or discomfort, their attachment system is activated. This prompts them to quickly turn towards their caretakers or use proximity-seeking behaviors such as crying, reaching out, calling out or, later, crawling and following their attachment figure. If the child receives the support, reassurance and comfort they need from their caretaker, their nervous system then returns to a state of calm homeostasis. Infants and children who can't yet fully regulate their own emotional states depend on their caretakers to co-regulate for them. Being close with another human helps children to feel calm. Further, being connected to and soothed by their caretakers over time teaches them how to self-soothe and regulate their own emotional states. As children, we want to know that our attachment figures are nearby and accessible. We need to know that they will provide us with a safe haven to turn to when we need them, which then gives us a secure base from which we can explore our environment. Bowlby called this the exploratory behavioral system. When our attachment needs are being met, this system enables us to feel comfortable and free to explore ourselves, others and the world around us.

John Bowlby and Mary Ainsworth's research shows that children develop attachment styles that are more secure or more insecure, depending on how well their parents are able to be a connected and responsive safe haven for them. If their caretakers are able to meet most of their needs enough of the time, children usually have a secure attachment. But if they experience their parents as inconsistent, inaccessible, unresponsive or even threatening and dangerous, they adapt by developing more insecure attachment styles. Table 1.1 summarizes how parental behaviors relate to childhood attachment styles.

Parental behaviors	Childhood attachment style
Protective, emotionally available, responsive, attuned	Secure
Unavailable, unresponsive, imperceptive or misattuned, rejecting	Avoidant
Inconsistently responsive, available or attuned; intrusive; acting out of their own needs for attention, affection or security over the child's needs	Anxious
Frightening, threatening, frightened, disorienting, alarming	Disorganized

TABLE 1.1: Summary chart of parental behaviors and childhood attachment styles

The following questions and exercises are designed to support you in understanding your childhood attachment experiences with your different attachment figures and how these formative experiences impacted you and shaped who you became. You may find that you have a mix of secure and insecure attachment experiences among your different attachment figures, or you may have had a blend of insecure and secure attachment experiences with the same attachment figure.

EXERCISE 1.1

In your childhood, who were your primary (or most significant) attachment figures? These may have been your biological parents, adopted parents, stepparents, grandparents, siblings, other family members, foster parents, mentors or others. Name them in the chart. Since you may have had less or more than four attachment figures, feel free to only use the columns you need, or use a separate sheet of paper if needed.

Attachment figure #1	Attachment figure #2	Attachment figure #3	Attachment figure #4

EXERCISE 1.2

Here are some childhood experiences that can lead to a child taking on more of a **secure** attachment style. You can fill in this chart in a couple of different ways. You can put a check mark in each box to indicate whether you did or did not experience the behavior with your attachment figure, or you could use a scale of 0 to 3 to rate your experiences on a spectrum.

0　Never experienced
1　Experienced less than 50% of the time
2　Experienced more than 50% of the time
3　Always (or close enough to always) experienced

If this person...	Figure #1	Figure #2	Figure #3	Figure #4
Was physically present and available to you				
Was able to keep you safe and protected				
Was attuned to your physical and emotional needs				
Responded appropriately and in a timely way to you when you needed help, support or attention				
Helped soothe and comfort you when you were upset, scared or angry				
Expressed delight in who you were (versus what you did or achieved)				
Encouraged you to be yourself				
Supported you to pursue your own interests and autonomy				
Celebrated your important milestones and achievements				
Helped prepare you for the challenges you would face or for being in the bigger world				
Played and laughed with you				
Repaired with you when they made mistakes				

EXERCISE 1.3

Here are some childhood experiences that can lead to deactivating your attachment needs and taking on more of an **avoidant or dismissive** attachment adaptation. You can put a check mark in each box to indicate whether you did or did not experience the behavior with your attachment figure, or you could use a scale of 0 to 3 to rate your experiences on a spectrum.

0 Never experienced
1 Experienced less than 50% of the time
2 Experienced more than 50% of the time
3 Always (or close enough to always) experienced

If this person…	Figure #1	Figure #2	Figure #3	Figure #4
Was physically absent or gone for long periods of time				
Was not attuned (or was misattuned) to your physical and emotional needs				
Was emotionally cold, rejecting or disconnected				
Was more focused on work, other people or other situations than on you				
Was not available to comfort you when you were upset, scared or angry				
Minimized or was unresponsive when you were struggling or when you had something to celebrate				
Was over-responsive (i.e., became angry, intrusive, intense or emotionally big) to your experiences in a way that felt like too much for you				
Offered little to no touch or affection				
Was critical, judgmental, dismissing or minimizing of you and your experiences				
Focused on what you achieved or how you appeared to others				
Encouraged you (whether explicitly or implicitly) to be more self-reliant and independent				
Expected you to know how to do things that were beyond your years and developmental capacity				
Was unable to really get you or understand you				
Was too strict, controlling or rigid				

Reflection Questions

Can you recall a situation with your childhood primary attachment figure in which you felt the need to withdraw or minimize your attachment needs?

....

....

....

....

....

....

....

Can you recall times when having fewer needs and being more independent was reinforced or rewarded in your family or culture?

....

....

....

....

....

....

....

What beliefs about yourself and others did you take away from these experiences?

....

....

....

....

....

....

How has this attachment strategy shown up for you as an adult?

....

....

....

....

....

....

EXERCISE 1.4

Here are some childhood experiences that can lead to hyperactivating your attachment needs and taking on more of an **anxious or preoccupied** attachment adaptation. You can put a check mark in each box to indicate whether you did or did not experience the behavior with your attachment figure, or you could use a scale of 0 to 3 to rate your experiences on a spectrum.

0   Never experienced
1   Experienced less than 50% of the time
2   Experienced more than 50% of the time
3   Always (or close enough to always) experienced

If this person...	Figure #1	Figure #2	Figure #3	Figure #4
Was unreliable, inconsistent or unpredictable in how they showed up for you when you needed help, support or attention				
Acted in ways that left you feeling anxious about who you were				
Acted in ways that left you feeling anxious about their abilities as a parent or that you had to be hyper-focused on what they were doing and their state of mind				
Conveyed messages that you were responsible for their feelings or needs				
Punished, criticized or guilt-tripped you about your independence, autonomy or curiosity				
Was a "helicopter parent," which may have included excessive praise, control or perfectionist standards				
Responded to you only once you got louder, emotionally bigger, more upset or emotionally dysregulated				
Was inconsistent in setting and maintaining boundaries				

Reflection Questions

Can you recall a situation with your childhood primary attachment figure in which you felt anxious and uncertain about whether your attachment needs would be met?

....

....

....

....

....

....

Can you recall a situation with your childhood primary attachment figure in which you felt heightened or anxious behavior was the only way to elicit a response or affection from them?

....

....

....

....

....

....

What beliefs about yourself and others did you take away from these experiences?

....

....

....

....

....

....

How has this attachment strategy shown up as an adult?

....

....

....

....

....

....

....

EXERCISE 1.5

In addition to the attachment experiences you may have already stated in responding to the reflection questions above about the other two insecure attachment styles, here are some additional childhood experiences that can lead to taking on more of a **disorganized, fearful or avoidant** attachment adaptation.

If this person...	✓ Check the boxes for each attachment figure			
	Figure #1	Figure #2	Figure #3	Figure #4
Was physically, emotionally or sexually abusive to you				
Was physically, emotionally or sexually abusive to others in front of you in the same home				
Was neglectful to the point that you were left unprotected in critical times				
Was addicted to drugs or alcohol				
Was hostile, humiliating, scary or threatening in their responses to you				
Conveyed messages that you were not enough, or that you were incapable, stupid or failing in some way				
Was in constant or repeated crisis				
Was incarcerated or engaged with dangerous or illegal activities				

Reflection Questions

If you checked off experiences in the above chart, how did this impact your sense of safety and security?

_____

_____

_____

_____

_____

What beliefs about yourself and others did you take away from these experiences?

_____

_____

_____

_____

_____

How has this attachment strategy shown up as an adult?

_____

_____

_____

_____

_____

EXERCISE 1.6

Overall Reflection Questions

What did *all* of these experiences teach you about:

Whether or not you were worthy of love and attention?

....

....

....

....

....

Whether your needs were welcome, allowed, not allowed
or forbidden?

....

....

....

....

....

Setting boundaries and saying no?

....

....

....

....

....

How did these experiences shape:

Your self-esteem?

....

....

....

....

....

Your perception of who you were and what you were capable of?

....

....

....

....

....

Your ability to self-regulate?

....

....

....

....

....

Your ability to co-regulate?

....

....

....

....

....

What did these experiences teach you about how much or how little:

You could trust others?

....

....

....

....

....

You could ask for help?

....

....

....

....

....

You could depend on and rely on others?

....

....

....

....

....

You could share your inner thoughts and feelings with others?

....

....

....

....

....

You could share your hopes and dreams with others?

....

....

....

....

....

Even when we have experienced insecure attachment histories, we
often gain many strengths from these painful experiences.
What are some of the strengths that you gained from the
experiences you went through?

....

....

....

....

....

What were some of the people or factors in your life that aided you in your resilience to your past hardships, neglects and trauma?

....

....

....

....

....

What are the ways that you have been positively shaped by these experiences in terms of the values, qualities and capacities that you now have as an adult?

....

....

....

....

....

....

CHAPTER TWO

THE DIFFERENT DIMENSIONS OF ATTACHMENT

Most attachment researchers base their work on the idea of categorizing people under one of four specific types: secure, preoccupied, dismissive or fearful-avoidant. More recently, however, some researchers have proposed that attachment is better described using the two dimensions of attachment anxiety and attachment avoidance, and looking at the different ways these dimensions can interact. They place each of these dimensions along an axis from high to low, and then cross the axes to form a diagram with four quadrants. While this model still produces the same four basic types (one per quadrant), it lets us see a few things in more nuanced ways based on how far along each axis we find ourselves.

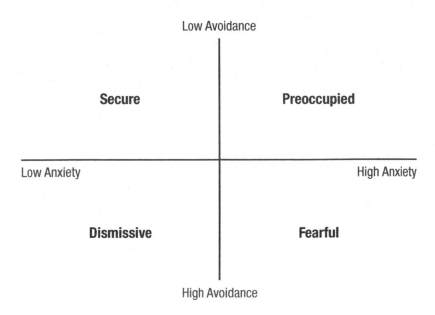

FIGURE 2.1: Dimensions of attachment

EXERCISE 2.1

Based on the chart showing the relationship between the dimensions of attachment anxiety and attachment avoidance in your **childhood**, when thinking of your relationships with each of your different attachment figures from childhood, where would you place yourself on this chart? (You may place yourself in different locations, depending on which childhood attachment figure you are reflecting on.)

What about your experience in each relationship contributed to you being higher or lower in attachment avoidance?

....

....

....

....

....

....

....

What about your experience in each relationship contributed to you being higher or lower in attachment anxiety?

....

....

....

....

....

....

....

EXERCISE 2.2

Based on the chart showing the relationship between the dimensions of attachment anxiety and attachment avoidance in your **adulthood**, who would you consider to be your attachment-based relationships (romantic, non-romantic, sexual or platonic)?

When thinking of your relationships with different attachment figures from adulthood, where would you place yourself on this chart for each of these relationships? What about your experience in each relationship contributed to you being higher or lower in attachment avoidance?

What about your experience in each relationship contributed to you being higher or lower in attachment anxiety?

If the relationship is current, what can you do to experience less attachment anxiety or attachment avoidance?

....

....

....

....

....

....

What can you ask for from the other people in this relationship that would support you in experiencing less attachment avoidance or attachment anxiety?

....

....

....

....

....

....

From Dysfunction to Desire

Another way to conceive of the attachment dimensions is not through their "dysfunctions," but through their strengths and desires. Each insecure attachment style comes with certain strengths and capacities that are important to acknowledge. The insecure attachment styles are not just survival strategies that kick into gear in response to attachment rupture or relationship distress. At their root, they can also be expressions of the essential human desires for autonomy and connection. On one hand we have the need for agency, independence and choice, and on the other hand we have the need for closeness, connection, support and union.

People with a higher draw to autonomy can exhibit more highly developed abilities for self-sufficiency and competence in tending to the practical, logistical and material aspects of the world. They have the ability to compartmentalize emotions, which can be a very handy skill in certain circumstances. When these needs move too far outside of their healthy expressions, agency and autonomy can transform into feeling alienation and isolation, becoming emotionally unreachable, or refusing or even denying the need for connection or help from others. A person's boundaries can get too rigid, and they may shut others out and shut themselves too far in.

People who are more aligned with the values of connection and togetherness can have highly developed skills when it comes to identifying and attuning to the emotions of others, and they can be highly competent in tending to others' needs and handling the responsibilities of interpersonal relationships. When this goes too far, straying from its healthy expression, a person's communing drives can become unhealthy forms of enmeshment and fusion. They may lose themselves in a relationship and see a decreased ability to truly know themselves or even make up their own minds. Figure 2.2 shows the spectrum of these states.

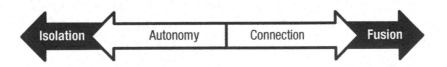

FIGURE 2.2: The spectrum of autonomy and connection

EXERCISE 2.3

When you think of the different important attachment relationships in your life from childhood and adulthood, where would you place yourself on this spectrum of isolation and fusion (Fig. 2.2)?

In general, do you tend towards one side of this spectrum over the other? Or has your position changed based on the relationship or on different life circumstances?

Think about different types of relationships in your life, such as relationships with your friends, co-workers, parents, children, superiors, mentors, teachers, *metamours*, lovers, and so on. How does where you would place yourself on this spectrum change based on these different types of relationships, and why do you think that is?

What have your experiences of being more of the distancer in a relationship been like?

....

....

....

....

....

....

....

What have your experiences of being more of the pursuer in a relationship been like?

....

....

....

....

....

....

....

EXERCISE 2.4

Based on the idea that your attachment styles are not solely dysfunc-
tional, but instead are also expressions of understandable coping
strategies as well as representing different strengths, capacities and
desires, use the next two charts to answer the following prompts.

- List the different ways that you currently express your autonomy
  and connection in ways that feel less than ideal or healthy for you.
- List the ways that you can move too far into fusion or isolation.

Isolation	Autonomy	Connection	Fusion

- List the ways that you already express your autonomy in ways that feel healthy, supportive or nurturing to you.
- List the ways that you already express connection in ways that feel healthy, supportive or nurturing to you.

Isolation	Autonomy	Connection	Fusion

EXERCISE 2.5

In the chart below:
- List the ways that you can further increase your healthy expressions of autonomy and of connection.
- List the ways that you can prevent yourself from going too far into isolation or fusion.

Isolation	Autonomy	Connection	Fusion

Boundaries

Our boundaries are the ways we protect ourselves physically, mentally and emotionally. Our boundaries are the meeting point between ourselves and another—the point at which we can be both separate and connected. Our boundaries guide us in navigating our relationships and they are directly related to the ways in which we are able to give and receive love. When we've experienced attachment wounds as children or adults, we can experience disruptions in our ability to establish boundaries that are connected and protective, compromising our ability to give love, receive love or both. Table 2.1 shows the different ways that your boundaries can be expressed depending on how much emphasis you are putting on being connected with others as well as protected from others. Based on these two factors, our boundaries can be expressed as healthy, porous or rigid.

	Input	Output
Healthy Boundaries Being connected and protected.	We can connect with others, while also maintaining our sense of self. We can take in love from others.	We share our feelings, opinions and perspectives, while respecting and allowing others to be distinct and separate from us. We can give to others.
Porous Boundaries Being connected but not protected.	Over-receiving: We absorb and allow in what is not ours. We lose our sense of self.	Over-giving: We intrude onto others, inserting our thoughts, feelings, opinions, perspectives or sense of self into them.
Rigid Boundaries Being protected but not connected.	Under-receiving: We block out the input and love of others.	Under-giving: We restrain ourselves from expressing or giving to others.

TABLE 2.1: Boundary chart

EXERCISE 2.6

Use the following diagrams of a human body to draw what your boundaries look like. Have fun with different kinds of lines, shapes, colors, adjectives (i.e., sticky, sharp, soft, gooey, porous), you name it!

Some drawing ideas:

- Draw how far outside or inside of your body your output boundary is.
- Draw how far outside or inside of your body your input boundary is.
- Where do you have more porous boundaries? What color, shape or texture do these take?
- Where do you have more rigid boundaries? What color, shape or texture do these take?
- Draw what your boundaries used to look like compared to what they look like now.
- Draw what healthy boundaries of being protected and con-nected would look like for you.
- Draw your ideal boundary avatar on the blank page!

EXERCISE 2.7

Here are some general reflection questions about boundaries.

In what ways do you experience your boundaries as porous, whether by being absorbing, by being intrusive or both?

....

....

....

....

....

....

In what ways do you experience your boundaries as rigid, whether by blocking, by restraining or both?

....

....

....

....

....

....

....

To feel healthier in your boundaries, do you need to focus more on tightening up your boundaries and protecting yourself, whether on the input or output? What are some ideas about how you can do this?

_____

_____

_____

_____

_____

_____

Do you need to focus more on softening the rigidity of your boundaries and allowing more connection, whether on the input or output? What are some ideas about how you can do this?

_____

_____

_____

_____

_____

_____

EXERCISE 2.8

Reflect on a relationship where you would like your boundaries to be different.

How do you find yourself over-giving in this relationship? What beliefs about yourself play into this? What beliefs about others play into this?

....

....

....

....

....

....

....

How do you find yourself under-giving in this relationship? What beliefs about yourself play into this? What beliefs about others play into this?

....

....

....

....

....

....

....

In what ways do you find yourself over-receiving or over-taking in this relationship? What beliefs about yourself or about others play into this?

In what ways do you find yourself under-receiving in this relationship? What beliefs about yourself or about others play into this?

What would the ideal version of yourself look like in this relationship
in terms of boundaries? What would giving and receiving look like
for this version of yourself?

....

....

....

....

....

....

....

What requests would you like to make of this person about
respecting your boundaries?

....

....

....

....

....

....

....

CHAPTER THREE

THE NESTED MODEL OF ATTACHMENT AND TRAUMA

In this chapter, I offer an additional perspective to our discussion of attachment in an attempt to diversify the levels or dimensions at which we consider and contemplate our attachment experiences. Attachment unfolds over multiple levels of the human experience. When referring to different levels of experience, I am pointing to the different dimensions or aspects of our human experience: self, relationships, home, local communities and culture, society, and the global or collective. These different levels may seem separate and distinct from one another, yet they are all interconnected, with each level acting as an important ingredient of our overall experience of life and informing every moment as well as the decisions we make. These levels or dimensions are not intended to refer to a hierarchy where one level is better, worse, or more or less important than the other, but as we move from the self all the way to the global, the levels do increase in complexity when it comes to both our internal and external experiences.

FIGURE 3.1: The nested model of attachment and trauma

EXERCISE 3.1

For this section you will explore what each of these levels means to you, as well as the different pains and supports that you have experienced at each of these levels. In Chapter Six, we will look at the nested model of attachment and trauma specifically applied to your experiences with nonmonogamy, so I recommend that in this section you answer the questions in a more general way or in relationship to another important aspect of your identity (i.e., race, gender, class, body ability, sexual orientation, religion and so on).

Self

What ten words would you use to describe yourself?

....

....

....

....

What are the qualities about yourself that make you smile?

....

....

....

....

What are some of your skills and capacities that you are grateful for?

....

....

....

....

What are the qualities about yourself that you feel challenged by?

What are some new skills or capacities that you would like
to develop?

Are there certain typologies—such as your astrology, Myers-Briggs
personality type, Enneagram number, Human Design, archetypes,
and so on—that you think describe you well? Explain.

What are your top most important identities (i.e., sex, gender,
religion, sexual orientation, occupation, family roles and others)?

Which aspects of yourself fit within a majority group or privileged norm?

....

....

....

....

Which aspects of yourself are outside of a majority group or privileged norm?

....

....

....

....

How do your answers to both of these last two questions shape how you see yourself?

....

....

....

....

What are some hardships that you've experienced that you have risen above or healed from? How did you do this?

....

....

....

....

What are some of the ways that you currently struggle with yourself? (For instance: I procrastinate, I judge my body, I'm a perfectionist...)

....

....

....

....

Which qualities, skills or capacities that you mentioned above can you apply to the ways you currently struggle with yourself?

....

....

....

....

If there was a movie made about your life, which actor would play you or which superhero would you be?

....

....

....

....

Relationships

As listed in Chapter One, who were your primary attachment figures in childhood?

....

....

....

....

Did your attachment style with any of these attachment figures
change through the years? What initiated the change?

....

....

....

....

....

If you had siblings, what was your attachment experience like
with them?

....

....

....

....

....

Who were the important friends that you had growing up?

....

....

....

....

Were there any pets, fictional characters or inanimate objects that
were important attachments for you?* Describe them.

....

....

....

....

....

---

* Our attachments do not only have to be with humans. Animals and humans
can have strong attachment bonds and imaginary friends, fictional characters,
celebrities we've never met and even inanimate objects can also become
objects of attachment and affection.

What were the main hardships, attachment ruptures, violations or losses that you experienced at this relational level?

_____

_____

_____

_____

_____

Who were the people that taught you about what you value most in life?

_____

_____

_____

_____

_____

Who were the people that you felt the most safe and secure with?

_____

_____

_____

_____

_____

In what ways do you show up as a safe and secure person for others?

_____

_____

_____

_____

_____

Are there any relationships, past or present, that need your forgiveness or repair? Forgiveness or repair may not be appropriate or possible for every relationship that has experienced ruptures or estrangement. For a relationship that you believe can be mended or that you would like to see repaired, what steps can you take towards restoring this relationship?

....

....

....

....

....

Home

How many homes did you live in as a child?

....

....

....

....

....

Did you like your home(s)? Did you feel safe there?

....

....

....

....

....

Describe your sleeping arrangements or what your room was like, if you had one.

_____

_____

_____

_____

Was the physical environment of your home something that mattered to you?

_____

_____

_____

_____

Where in your home did you feel the most comfortable and relaxed?

_____

_____

_____

_____

How many people were living in your home?

_____

_____

_____

_____

How did they treat each other? How did this affect you?

....

....

....

....

....

Did you feel safe to be yourself in your home?

....

....

....

....

....

What were the main hardships, attachment ruptures, traumas or losses that you experienced at this level?

....

....

....

....

....

Today, how do you feel about where you live?

....

....

....

....

....

Is your current home a place where you can relax?

....

....

....

....

....

Does the way your home is set up, organized or decorated represent who you are and what matters to you? How could your home be a more fulfilling or accurate expression of who you are, as well as any other people that you live with?

....

....

....

....

....

Local communities and culture

As a child, where were the primary places that you spent time outside of your home (i.e., school, friends' homes, religious centers, after-school clubs)?

....

....

....

....

....

Did you feel safe in your neighborhood?

....

....

....

....

When you were growing up, how did your school culture affect your feelings of safety and security and your ability to explore?

....

....

....

....

What communities and cultures were you and your family a part of?

....

....

....

....

What did these communities and cultures teach you about who you were supposed to be and who you were not supposed to be?

....

....

....

....

Did you feel accepted in these different communities?

_____

_____

_____

_____

_____

Were there ways you tried to change who you were in order to fit in?
How did this impact you?

_____

_____

_____

_____

_____

What were the main hardships, attachment ruptures, traumas or
losses that you experienced within your local culture or community?

_____

_____

_____

_____

_____

Were there ways that you felt embraced and accepted by certain
cultures or communities? How did this impact you?

_____

_____

_____

_____

Today, what are the communities and cultures that you most
identify with?

....

....

....

....

....

Are there certain cultural norms or communities that you would
benefit from stepping away from? How would you describe these?

....

....

....

....

....

Where have you found healing at this nested level of community
and culture?

....

....

....

....

....

In what ways can you bring more community and culture into your
life or deepen your experience in the communities and cultures you
are already a part of?

....

....

....

....

....

Technology†

How did technology affect your family home?

....

....

....

....

How has technology impacted your relationship with yourself?

....

....

....

....

How has your use of technology hindered your ability to connect with others?

....

....

....

....

---

† Technology is a dimension of our lives that impacts and spans all of the different nested levels. I choose to place it under "local communities and culture" because of the ways I've seen technology change the communities and cultures that we have access to, create new communities and cultures that previously did not exist, and change how we relate and attach to our existing and new communities. However, as my questions imply, I also acknowledge the significant impact technology can have on the other nested levels. You may personally find that for you, technology has had a bigger impact on a different dimension of the nested model and that it can be both positive or negative depending on the nested level or even within the same level.

How has your use of technology enhanced your ability to connect with others?

....

....

....

....

How has your use of technology impacted the ways that you attach and bond with others?

....

....

....

....

Have any virtual communities contributed to you having more secure or insecure attachment experiences? Which ones and how?

....

....

....

....

How has technology impacted your connection with the social or global nested levels?

....

....

....

....

Social

This refers to the larger social structures, systems and institutions (i.e., economic, legal, political, medical, religious) that you have operated within and that have shaped your life experience. What social system or institutions did you experience growing up?

How have you experienced privilege or increased access or opportunity within social structures, systems and institutions?

How have you experienced wounding or discrimination within social structures, systems and institutions?

Have you gained or lost rights or privileges in your lifetime?

How has your race, class, religion, gender identity or sexual identity
impacted your ability to bond, attach or connect with others?

....

....

....

....

....

Global or collective

What is your relationship to nature?

....

....

....

....

....

How do you find connection and healing there, if at all?

....

....

....

....

....

How has the earth "betrayed" you? For instance, perhaps
you've had traumatic experiences such as hurricanes, fires or
other disasters.

....

....

....

....

....

Do you come from a lineage in which people have experienced famine, oppression, slavery or genocide? If so, how has this impacted your understanding of yourself and the world?

_____

_____

_____

_____

_____

Do you come from a lineage in which people have been colonizers, wartime aggressors, exploitative rulers or race- or class-based oppressors? If so, how has this impacted your understanding of yourself and the world?

_____

_____

_____

_____

_____

The Multigenerational Impact of Attachment

By focusing on your attachment history through the exercise and questions you've gone through thus far, it can be easy to feel like a victim, to be angry, and to blame your parents and the world for unjust, unfair, painful and traumatic experiences in your life. In the next section I will talk about the importance of accepting our own individual past, but I first want to emphasize the importance of acknowledging the multigenerational attachment experiences that our parents had with their own parents, what our grandparents experienced with their parents and so on.

When I was a teenager, I was extremely angry at both of my parents for their inability to provide the protection, presence and attunement that I needed. I was becoming guarded and righteous because of it and every other adult and family member in my life validated that I was justified in being so. When I started to learn more about the hardships and traumas that my parents went through when they were younger, as well as my grandparents' histories, I softened. Both my parents experienced different forms of physical and emotional abuse, neglect and significant loss. As young adults they found refuge in addiction to drugs, alcohol or love and romance. My grandparents each had their own set of hardships that could fill an entire novel, and given the era that they grew up in and the parenting advice that was available to them then, I could grasp and even appreciate why they were the way they were. As I dug into their stories, I could see the multigenerational patterns of attachment insecurity and I was able to more fully understand what made them act in the ways they did. It didn't excuse how they behaved with me, but it put their parenting and grandparenting into a fuller context.

I do not believe that forgiveness is something that we have to *do*—an action or practice that we have to work diligently at in order to accomplish. And in many cases, forgiveness of those who have harmed us may not be fitting or appropriate. No one should be pressured to forgive the people, communities or institutions that have harmed them. Adages like "forgive and forget" can be dismissive and silencing of the people who have been harmed, or even make victims responsible for protecting or absolving those that have harmed them. With that said, in some situations, forgiveness is warranted. This can be true in certain cases where people have taken responsibility for their actions and are genuinely seeking repair, or in situations when we understand that someone caused harm but did not intend to. It can also apply at times when people demonstrate that they have grown and changed for the better, or when *we* are the one who honestly wants to forgive—not because we have been coerced and guilted to forgive, but because we wholeheartedly want to.

When forgiveness is relevant, I believe that it can be a natural byproduct of *understanding* instead of something that we have to actively achieve. When we can step into another person's shoes and comprehend the factors that led them to make the choices they did— again, not as an excuse—our perspective can expand beyond our own and we realize that we are not actually alone in our pain and suffering. Trauma and attachment insecurities are often unintentionally passed down from one generation to the next, making us the inheritor of a familial as well as a socio-political legacy that robs people of their power and separates them from their capacity to love.

EXERCISE 3.2

What do you know about the hardships, losses, pains and traumas
that your parents went through? Use the nested model to consider
the multi-level aspects of their upbringing.

....

....

....

....

....

....

....

....

How about your grandparents or even great-grandparents? Use the
nested model to consider the multi-level aspects of their upbringing.

....

....

....

....

....

....

....

....

If you don't know the history and life circumstances of your parents, can you imagine what their life might have been like that led them to make the choices they made that you do know about?

EXERCISE 3.3

I call this exercise "Stepping into their shoes." You can do this exercise as a visualization with your eyes closed, or a writing exercise in your journal. Or you can literally go take a walk outside or walk around your home, pretending that you are walking in the shoes of one of your parents or grandparents for a few minutes, as if you were them. You can do this exercise more than once for each of your different relatives. I would recommend allowing some space and time between each person you do this exercise for.

- Given what you know or can at least imagine about your parent's or grandparent's life and their attachment experiences, take a few minutes to step into their shoes. Imagine what it would have been like to be them. What factors from the nested model were they born into? How were they treated by their parents and other relatives? How did they see the world? How did they see others in their life? What were some of their hopes and dreams? What were their pains, struggles, insecurities and confusions? How did this influence them and their capacity to be present, available and attuned as a parent or grandparent?
- Step out of their shoes and fully return back to yourself.
- Optional step: As the present-moment adult you, imagine that the person you just did this exercise for is standing in front of you and offer some kind words or sentiments to them (i.e., "May you be safe," "May you be happy and healthy," "I wish you the healing and security that you need," "I'm sorry that you went through what you did," or "May you experience your own love and empowerment"). Offering such statements in this exercise does not mean that you have to engage with this person any differently in real life, especially in cases where it is best for you to maintain distance from this person for your own mental, physical or emotional health and safety. Your statements can also be neutral, such as "I hope you find the help you need" if that is what feels best for you in this optional step.

EXERCISE 3.4

This is an exercise toward accepting your own past. As you go through these different exercises you are already taking many steps in the acknowledgment of your past experiences. Interestingly, I've found that many people have resistance to accepting their past. They are afraid that accepting their past is the same as indulging in it or that it will mean they have to over-identify with it. Accepting your past, what happened to you and what didn't happen for you, does not mean that you condone it. Accepting your past does not mean that you liked it, agreed with it or wanted it to happen. Accepting your history of attachment insecurity does not mean that you have to now take it on as an identity that you're stuck with. It just means that you acknowledge what you went through and are willing to take responsibility for who you are because of it.

For some of us, it may be very true that we were victimized or mistreated in childhood and that this had a big impact on who we are, but if we continue to use our past as an excuse for our adult behaviors now, we can easily perpetually dwell in our childhood and our insecure attachment styles that no longer serve us as they once did. For others, we may not be putting enough emphasis on our past and are actually avoiding accepting what we've previously gone through by minimizing or downplaying it. Saying things like "It wasn't that bad," "It could have been worse," or "Others had it worse than me" can be examples of being in denial about how our attachment needs were not sufficiently met. De-emphasizing our past can just be the other side of the same coin of over-emphasizing our past, which also makes us less likely to take responsibility for how we might still be playing out our previous insecure attachment experiences in our adult life today.

Accepting our past and acknowledging the pain and hardships that we went through is also not an indication of resignation or defeat. It is a way to reclaim ourselves, our power and our voice from our past—no longer being trapped by our reactivity, avoidance, denial, justifications or defensiveness. This frees us up to choose how we want to respond, attach and love.

EXERCISE 3.5

In this exercise, you'll create your own acceptance and acknowledgment statements. Come up with a single sentence that acknowledges and sums up your history. You can do this as a general statement or you can make more specific statements for each of your different attachment figures. Or you can do both! Try to make this a *matter-of-fact* statement about your experience.

Some examples are:

- General: I experienced multiple forms of abuse, neglect and poverty as a child, which was really hard for me.
- General: I was lucky to have my physical and financial needs met, but I did not have my emotional needs met as a child.
- General: I experienced neglect as a child, and this left me feeling lonely and like I can't trust others to be there for me.
- General: Because of my race and sexual orientation, I felt invisible growing up and I never felt like I fit into the world around me.
- Specific: My mom emphasized perfectionism and frequently criticized me, so I now struggle with over-achieving and low self-esteem.
- Specific: My father left us for another family so I struggle with trusting that others will stay and not leave.
- Specific: My parents were highly focused on their careers and I often felt like I didn't matter to them.
- Specific: I'm one of six siblings, two of which had special needs, so even though I know my mom loved me, she was not able to give me the level of attention that I needed.

I suggest first writing out your statement, then saying it aloud to yourself. Some people feel very little as they craft and speak these statements, others can feel a lot. Clients of mine who have done this exercise report back that they usually like to work with these statements over several days, weeks, sometimes even months. If you'd like, you can also share your statements with a trusted person in your life. If you do share these statements with someone else, request that the listener is fully present for your sharing and reply with something simple like, "I really hear that you went through that," "Thank you for sharing," or "I'm sorry that this was your experience."

EXERCISE 3.6

This exercise will help you to have a "get it out" experience. As mentioned above, exploring our attachment history can understandably bring up difficult feelings. When we confront our past, feelings of grief, hopelessness and anger are normal. It's important to have ways to process and express these feelings so that they don't fester, pressurize and toxify inside us. Many of us have what I call a *backlog* of emotions that we need to release in order to be fully present in our lives.

If you feel that you have a backlog of anger or grief that you would like to release, below are suggestions for some "get it out" type of experiences. Please note that your intention for this matters! Releasing your emotional backlog is not just having a catharsis that causes you to either re-live your pain in ways that feel damaging or venting your anger in ways that just add more fuel to the fire. I suggest holding the intention of "off-gassing" your grief or anger by giving it a channel that truly feels like a helpful outlet and release—again, not just a re-triggering. Of course, not everything I suggest here is possible or appropriate for every person. Please only try out the exercises that feel safe, doable and supportive to you in this process.

Possible "off-gassing" exercises:
- Write it out! Write a letter to someone you've been hurt by. You won't actually send this letter, so don't hold back. Be as specific, profane and petty as you can be in writing out all the times and ways that you've felt hurt and angry in this relationship. Keep returning to your intention to be off-gassing and getting the anger and hurt out of your system, versus writing to reinforce an angry or victim perspective. When you're done with the letter, do something to destroy it as the next step in further letting go of these feelings. You can rip the letter up, burn it into ashes or find any other way that symbolizes the transformation of these feelings.
- Talk it out! Use the same instructions as above for writing it out, but speak what you want to say instead. You can record it and delete it; you can imagine that the person you're talking to is in front of you; you can ask a friend, therapist or coach to hold space for you and listen to you while you do this exercise; or you

can speak it to the sky. Talk it out in whatever way makes sense to you.

- Punch it out! Go to a boxing class, get a punching bag or use your mattress as a way to punch and move your anger and hurt out of your body.
- Shake it out! You can do this with or without music, but begin by thinking about the grief, hurt or pain that you are wanting to expel, feel it in your body and then dance or shake it off.
- Seek out a Somatic Experiencing practitioner who can help you move any stuck energy from your body.
- Go to a Rage Room, batting cage or golf range near you and have fun smashing away.
- Go into the woods or some private place in nature and break sticks. Conjure up what you are trying to release and imagine that every time you break a stick, more and more of what you are trying to release is being liberated. Making noises while you do this can feel empowering and support the process.
- Go to a grief retreat. Even if your losses took place many years ago, it can still be helpful to attend a grief workshop or retreat. Grief retreats are typically designed to provide a safe space for participants to actively grieve, be witnessed in their grief, and gain more tools to cope with the grieving and healing process.

Part *Two*

CHAPTER FOUR
CONSENSUAL NONMONOGAMY

Your *Why*

My experience with nonmonogamous clients has shown me that the people who articulate their deeper purpose—that is, their *why* for being nonmonogamous—are then better able to navigate the ups and downs that lie ahead. When the waters of consensual nonmonogamy (CNM) begin to pick up and the emotional rapids of opening up your relationship begin, having your *why* to remember and return to can serve as the needed life jacket that keeps you and your relationship afloat.

EXERCISE 4.1

Polysecure discusses a number of reasons why people choose CNM (p. 105–109). Write about how each of these reasons, listed below, does or does not relate to your *why* for choosing CNM:

Increased need fulfillment through having multiple partners

....

....

....

....

Having more variety of non-sexual activities

....

....

....

....

Increased personal growth

....

....

....

....

....

Sexual

Philosophical

Being CNM by orientation

Do you have other reasons for practicing CNM that aren't mentioned here? If so, expand on these reasons.

Different Types of CNM

Figure 4.1 maps out the various types of CNM in terms of their relative degrees of sexual and emotional exclusivity.

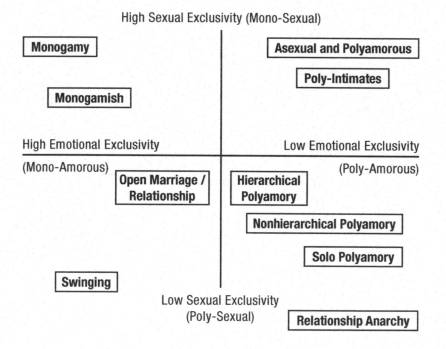

FIGURE 4.1: The different types of nonmonogamy

EXERCISE 4.2

Place yourself on this chart, based on your own values and desires around CNM. Where would you put your previous and current relationships on this chart? The placement of the different CNM styles in Figure 4.1 are suggestions. You might use the same term to describe your relationship style, but you would place it in a different location, so feel free to veer away from the chart in order to best represent what each style means to you. Have fun using post-its, stickers or different symbols for you and your partners.

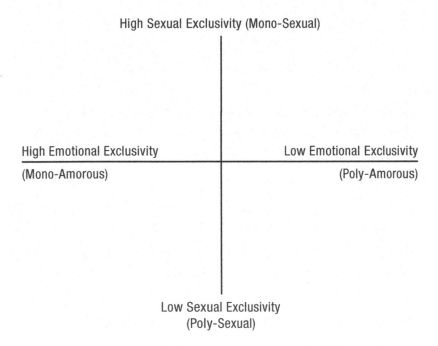

EXERCISE 4.3

Here are some reflection questions with regard to the chart you just filled out.

How has your place on the chart changed over time or depending on the other partners you've been with?

....

....

....

....

Do you see any relationship between the difficulty or ease you've experienced in certain relationships based on how close or far apart you each are placed on this chart?

....

....

....

....

Are certain types of CNM more or less preferable to you? Why?

....

....

....

....

....

When you are in a more secure attachment style, where would you place yourself on this chart?

....

....

....

....

....

When you are in a more insecure attachment style, where would you place yourself on this chart?

....

....

....

....

....

Are there other types, words, definitions or styles of CNM that you would use to describe your style of relating?

....

....

....

....

....

CHAPTER FIVE
ATTACHMENT AND NONMONOGAMY

Attachment research and resources for consensually nonmonog-amous relationships are scarce, as the field of attachment theory is highly *mononormative*. Research tends to assume monogamy, while resources tend to outright prescribe monogamy as the way to achieve secure attachment. Additionally, as some proponents of attachment theory assert that certain behaviors are shown to be associated with insecure attachment (i.e., casual sex, sex outside of marriage, sexting, BDSM), people then incorrectly assume that partaking in these behav-iors, which are more common among people practicing CNM, is an indication of insecure attachment. Because of this, many people prac-ticing CNM feel excluded from attachment theory and pathologized for their lifestyle or way of being.

Thankfully, the current research on CNM and attachment demon-strates that people in CNM relationships are just as likely to be securely attached as people in monogamous relationships, and in some cases people in polyamorous relationships are lower in attachment avoid-ance than people in monogamous relationships. Research has also shown that people with more than one partner exhibit secure attach-ment styles with each of their partners and that having an insecure attachment style with one partner did not affect the attachment style with the other partner, meaning that polyamorous adults can have different attachment styles with each of their partners that are independent of each other. This is similar to how children can have different attachment styles with their different attachment figures, as well as how monogamous adults can have different attachment styles from one relationship to the next or even change attachment styles within the same relationship over time.

When it comes to advice and resources on how to cultivate secure attachment in CNM relationships, up until this point the literature has been practically nonexistent. What has been available advises readers to rely heavily on structure and hierarchy in CNM relationships in order to achieve secure attachment instead of focusing on the quality of relating between partners. When we rely on the structure of our relationship, whether through being monogamous with someone or practicing hierarchical forms of CNM, we run the risk of forgetting that secure attachment is an embodied expression built upon how we consistently respond and attune to each other, not something that gets created through structure and hierarchy. Secure attachment is created through the quality of experience we have with our partners, not through the notion or the fact of either being married or being a primary partner.

We often assume that having more structural ties in a relationship means more security. In some cases it does, but as the high rates of divorce and cheating demonstrate, even a monogamous marriage that typically represents the pinnacle of relationship security is not necessarily any more secure than other forms of relationship. I've witnessed many couples who have measured their sense of personal and relationship security based on having shared finances, being legally married, running a business together, co-owning a home or counting how many carats the engagement ring has. These more structural demonstrations of security can be signs of genuine commitment and they undoubtedly make it more difficult for someone to just pick up and leave one day, but they do not ensure the high-quality attunement, presence and responsiveness that foster secure attachment at the interpersonal level.

EXERCISE 5.1

Here are some reflection questions on the topic of attachment theory itself.

Have you experienced feeling excluded or pathologized when learning about attachment theory or other psychological models? What were those experiences like for you?

_____

_____

_____

_____

_____

_____

_____

Have therapists, medical or mental health practitioners, or even friends and family tried to tell you that your sexual or relationship style is a form of dysfunction or insecure attachment? From a non-reactive place (i.e., not just putting them down and ripping them a new one), what would you like to say to these people?

_____

_____

_____

_____

_____

_____

_____

Relying on Structure for Secure Attachment

Some of the ways that we experience increased structure in our relationships are through such things as legal marriage, ceremonial commitment, shared finances, living together, owning property or possessions together, having children together, owning pets together, running a business together, being emergency contacts for each other, being each other's beneficiaries or powers of attorney, and being publicly known to each other's family or work colleagues.

EXERCISE 5.2

Here are some reflection questions on structure and secure attachments.

Are there any additional ways of having more structural security that you would put on this list?

....

....

....

....

....

....

Pick one to three relationships you've had and reflect on which of these structural elements were helpful for your attachment security.

....

....

....

....

....

....

Which of these structural elements never actually gave you the attachment security you would have liked?

In your transition from monogamy to nonmonogamy, were you still holding onto any of these structures? If so, what did they represent to you?

Which relationship structures are still important to you now?

Here are some signs that might indicate that you are relying more on the structure of your relationship for your attachment and security needs than on the emotional experience of your relationship:

Check off the ones that you have experienced.

- ☐ You know that, in theory, your partner loves you and is ultimately committed to you, your marriage or your family, but you don't feel personally valued, seen or cherished.
- ☐ You share many forms of structural commitment with your partner, but don't have emotional or sexual intimacy (and one or both of you is not OK with that).
- ☐ When you ask your spouse or partner for more of their time or affection, they get defensive and point out all of the professional, financial or domestic things that they do to show their commitment.
- ☐ You often feel alone in your relationship even though you live together or are around each other a lot.
- ☐ You or your partner defer to gender stereotypes to make the absence of certain forms of emotional or sexual connection more tolerable, such as "that's just how men are" or "well, you know how women can be."
- ☐ In your relationship, the ideal of the marriage or the greater purpose of the family have become more important than the direct experience of how you treat each other.
- ☐ You're married or in a primary partnership, but feel like you're always getting the short end of the stick when it comes to your spouse or partner's time, affection and attention.
- ☐ You know your partner is committed to you, but you don't know if they actually like and enjoy being with you.

CHAPTER SIX

THE IMPORTANCE OF ATTACHMENT IN CONSENSUAL NONMONOGAMY

Secure attachment with multiple romantic partners *is* possible. Adults can and do have multiple securely attached relationships and when secure functioning is at play within CNM relationships, partners communicate well, trust each other, stick to their agreements and discuss wanted changes. They tend to have more *compersion* for their partners, they act respectfully towards their metamours and while they still do experience jealousy or envy, they are also able to support each other in the process of managing it.

However, this is not always the case for people practicing CNM. In my practice with CNM clients I began to notice two distinct camps: those who were mostly thriving and those who seemed to be barely surviving. I call these people who thrive with their multiple partners *polysecure*. This is the state of being both securely attached to multiple romantic partners and having enough internal security to be able to navigate the structural relationship insecurity inherent to nonmonogamy, as well as the increased complexity and uncertainty that occurs when having multiple partners and metamours. More succinctly, being polysecure is having secure attachment with yourself and with your multiple partners. Individuals and couples can experience several challenges when transitioning to CNM. Attachment insecurity arising as a result of being nonmonogamous is one of the main ways that can seriously disrupt a person's sense of self, as well as their inner and outer safety, in ways that can make being CNM feel unbearable and unsustainable.

When transitioning into nonmonogamy, people may experience challenges with their attachment system in several different ways.

❶ Going CNM can expose your individual attachment insecurity

EXERCISE 6.1

Here are some examples of signs that your transition to CNM has exposed your own attachment insecurity. Check off which of these you have experienced and then answer the reflection questions.

☐ You intellectually want to be nonmonogamous, but you're having trouble with getting on board emotionally.

☐ Even though your partner has been wonderful about meeting enough of your relationship needs and is doing a good job reassuring you that you matter to them, you still experience a roller-coaster of anxiety before or during the time they spend with other people or you start to withdraw to protect yourself.

☐ You intellectually want to feel compersion for your partner's positive experiences with others, but you keep interpreting them being with others as a sign of your deficiency.

☐ After opening up, you are flooded with many memories of your childhood experiences or past traumas.

☐ After opening up, you realize that you have patterns of emotional or relational avoidance or codependency.

Reflection questions:

When you transitioned to CNM, which of your past traumas or attachment insecurities became exposed?

....

....

....

....

....

....

....

How did these experiences impact you?

How did they change your understanding of yourself, your relationship history and what you needed?

In what ways was monogamy buffering you from your attachment insecurities?

❷ Going CNM can expose attachment insecurities in the relationship that is opening up

EXERCISE 6.2

Here are a few reflection questions about attachment insecurities while opening up.

If you transitioned to CNM from a monogamous relationship, what attachment insecurities became exposed for you? For your partner?

....

....

....

....

....

....

In what ways was monogamy acting as a stand-in for secure attachment in your relationship?

....

....

....

....

....

....

....

....

What have you learned about yourself and your partner
through this?

....

....

....

....

....

....

....

....

❸ CNM is more structurally insecure than monogamy

EXERCISE 6.3

*Here are a few reflection questions about the structural insecurity
of CNM.*

Was entering a relationship paradigm that is less structurally secure
than monogamy difficult for you? How so?

....

....

....

....

....

....

....

....

In what ways was the less secure structure of CNM a positive experience for you?

....

....

....

....

....

....

....

....

What aspects of the mono-romantic ideal did you enjoy no longer participating in?

....

....

....

....

....

....

....

....

❹ Having multiple partners can replicate the conditions of attachment insecurity

EXERCISE 6.4

Here are some reflection questions about how this replication may have felt for you.

Once you began practicing CNM, in what ways did you experience attachment needs not being met in your relationship because your partners had less availability, responsiveness or emotional engagement due to now having multiple partners?

How did this impact your attachment anxiety or avoidance?

If you opened up from a monogamous relationship, how did the attachment experiences between the two of you change? In what ways were things better? In what ways were things harder?

....

....

....

....

....

....

How did you experience your partners as being more or less emotionally safe due to being CNM?

....

....

....

....

....

....

⑤ CNM can activate the attachment system into *primal attachment panic*

EXERCISE 6.5

Primal attachment panic is when someone experiences high levels of stress, anxiety and sympathetic nervous system activation when they are emotionally or physically separate from their attachment figure or fear that their relationship with their attachment figure is in danger or threatened.

What has been your experience of having primal attachment panic? What did you think was happening to you before you knew that this is an understandable attachment experience?

What has been your experience of your partners having primal attachment panic? What did you think was happening for them? Did you judge them for their experience? How did their primal panic impact you?

---

❻ There can be a mismatch of attachment expectations.

EXERCISE 6.6

Here are some potential signs that your attachment needs are not being considered (or are being violated) in your relationships. Check off which of these experiences you've had (whether on the giving or receiving end), and then answer the reflection questions below.

☐ Your partner is inconsistently there for you when you need them.

☐ Your partner ignores, or responds inconsistently to, your texts, emails or calls.

☐ Your partner ignores your explicit requests for time together or they keep saying that they want to do things with you but provide little to no follow-through.

☐ Your partner does things that make you question whether you are accepted, appreciated or valued.

☐ Your partner is inconsistent about the information they share about themselves, other partners or sexual activity.

☐ Relationship or sexual agreements are being broken.

☐ Your partner uses their other partners as an excuse for their own behavior.

☐ Your partner uses criticism, defensiveness, contempt or stonewalling.

☐ Your feelings, needs or opinions are not heard or don't carry much weight.

☐ Despite what your partner says about how much they care about you or how they *don't* practice hierarchy, other partners are getting preferential treatment.

☐ Your partner is effusively affectionate over text, but uncomfortable with verbal or physical affection in person.

☐ You are giving more than you are receiving.

☐ You are being asked to keep your relationship secret or lie about your relationship in front of certain people.

☐ You get more information from your metamours pertaining to important things about your partner than you do from your actual partner.

Reflection questions

What additional ways have you experienced your attachment needs being violated or not considered in your relationships?

_____

_____

_____

_____

_____

_____

_____

In what additional ways have you violated or not considered your partners' attachment needs?

_____

_____

_____

_____

_____

_____

What have been your experiences of wanting more of an attachment-based relationship than your partner does? How did this impact you and the relationship? Did you show up with attachment anxiety, avoidance or both?

_____

_____

_____

_____

_____

_____

What have been your experiences of being with a partner who wants more of an attachment-based relationship than you do? How did this impact you and the relationship? Did you show up with attachment anxiety, avoidance or both?

....

....

....

....

....

....

Are there any relationships in your life (romantic or not) that you would like to renegotiate to make them either more or less attachment-based? What would this look like?

....

....

....

....

....

....

Moving forward, how will you deal with a mismatch of attachment expectations with new partners?

....

....

....

....

....

➐ cnm can create new attachment ruptures

Living nonmonogamously can create new ruptures and traumas over the multiple dimensions of human experience that are presented in the nested model of attachment and trauma. Some of these experiences are subtler, where difficulty and pain result from an accumulation of stressful experiences within the various levels, and other experiences are more overtly oppressive, traumatic or damaging to attachment. On the other hand, being nonmonogamous can also facilitate new positive experiences, growth and levels of healing that might not have been available to us otherwise.

EXERCISE 6.7

For each level in the nested model, shown once again here, what new attachment ruptures, traumas or stressors have you experienced and what new types of healing, new connections or positive experiences have you had? Answer in the chart following the nested model.

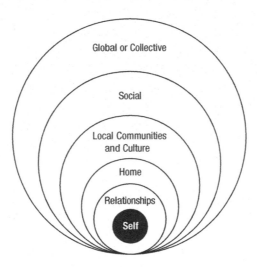

Nested level	New stressors, traumas or attachment ruptures	New healings, connections or positive experiences
Self		
Relationships		
Home		

Nested level	New stressors, traumas or attachment ruptures	New healings, connections or positive experiences
Local communities and culture		
Social		
Global or collective		

Part *Three*

CHAPTER SEVEN
THE FOUNDATIONS OF BEING POLYSECURE IN YOUR RELATIONSHIPS

In this chapter we explore the foundations of creating polysecurity with the partners with whom you want to be in an attachment-based relationship. Not all relationships or partners need to be attachment-based. We can have very fulfilling, meaningful, loving and significant relationships with people with whom we are less entwined, whom we don't want to label or define, or with whom we are not looking to actively build an attachment-based relationship. But when we are in attachment-based relationships, more is required, so the rest of this workbook will center on people who are (or want to be) in polyamorous attachment-based partnerships.

Do we want to be attachment-based partners?

The antecedent to being polysecure with your partners is first getting clear about whether you want to be attachment figures for each other. Our attachment-based relationships take time and investment, and so when referring to attachment-based partners I am referring to a choice that we are making to intentionally cultivate and tend to the attachment-based needs within a particular relationship. For us to feel safe and secure in our relationships, we need to know that our partners want to be there for us and will be to the best of their ability, and so some level of commitment to being in a relationship together is important. Depending on what stage of relationship you are in, this might look like:

- A commitment to staying in exploration of the relationship together, without specifically defining the future or integrating your lives.
- A commitment to building an official relationship in which you want to have longevity or be more interwoven.
- A commitment to building a life together where you are in it for the long haul.

Commitment can be expressed in many ways. Traditionally it is solidified through marriage, owning property, having kids or wearing certain types of jewelry, but legal, domestic or ornamental undertakings are not the only ways to show dedication.

EXERCISE 7.1

For past or current partners, which of these expressions of commitment did you experience or wish you had more of? As you fill out this table, think about how each expression of commitment helped or hindered your sense of secure attachment in each relationship.

Examples of demonstrations of commitment	Partner A	Partner B	Partner C	Partner D
Sharing intimate details (hopes, dreams, fears) and being vulnerable with each other				
Introducing each other to the important people in your lives				
Helping each other with practical or domestic tasks such as home or car maintenance, moving, cooking, taking care of children, helping with family members or pets, doing homework, job hunting, shopping, filing taxes and so on				
Having regular time together, both mundane and novel				
Making the person a priority (and defining what "making a priority" means to each of you)				
Planning trips together				
Being available to partners when they are sick or in need				
Collaborating on projects together				
Having frequent communication				

Examples of demonstrations of commitment	Partner A	Partner B	Partner C	Partner D
Add your own!				

EXERCISE 7.2

Here are some reflection questions to answer for yourself.

What other ways not listed do you express your commitment to your partners?

....

....

....

....

....

....

How do your partners show their commitment to you?

....

....

....

....

....

....

What does commitment mean to you?

....

....

....

....

....

....

What aspects of commitment are most important to you—structural, emotional or public?

....

....

....

....

....

....

Partner Exercise

And here are some questions to answer with your current or future partners:

Why do we want to be attachment figures for each other?

What does being an attachment figure look like for each of us?

What expectations do we have about how available, responsive and emotionally engaged we want our partners to be?

What are clear ways that we can each express our commitment?

....

....

....

....

....

....

What behaviors would be violations of our commitment to
each other?

....

....

....

....

....

Do we each have time and availability to offer this level
of involvement?

....

....

....

....

....

....

Once you are clear that being an attachment figure is what each of you wants, whether in a two-person or multi-person relationship, figuring out how to do this securely is the next step. Being a safe haven and a secure base for each other as partners is key for being polysecure.

Being a Safe Haven for Each Other

The bedrock of being polysecure in our relationships is feeling that we have a safe haven to turn to. This happens when our partners care about our safety, seek to respond to our distress, help us to co-regulate and soothe, and are a source of emotional and physical support and comfort. Similarly, when our partners are struggling or in need, we can be a safe haven by being there for them in warm, caring and receptive ways. We ultimately want to know that we are seen, heard and valued by our partners.

In our safe haven relationships, we want positive answers to questions such as:

- If I turn towards you, will you be there for me?
- Will you receive and accept me instead of attack, criticize, dismiss or judge me?
- Will you help comfort me?
- Will you respond in a way that calms my nervous system?
- Do I matter to you?
- Do I make a difference in your life?
- Can we lean into and rely on each other?

Here are some examples of things that you and your partners can do to be safe havens for each other:

- Give emotional support and comfort.
- Listen to each other with full attention.
- Inquire and share about feelings and needs.
- Track what is going on in each other's lives and make sure to follow up and inquire about those things.
- Help in practical ways when a partner is tired or sick.
- Discuss or debrief events of the day or things that are important to each of you.
- Let your partners know how and why they matter to you.

EXERCISE 7.3

In each of your attachment-based relationships or for the relationships that you would like to see become more attachment-based, ask yourself:

How does this partner already act as a safe haven for me?

....

....

....

....

....

....

In what ways do they show up for me that feel supportive and comforting?

....

....

....

....

....

....

How can this partner help me feel even more safe with them?

....

....

....

....

....

....

How can this partner help me feel even more supported or comforted by them, in general or in specific situations?

....

....

....

....

....

....

In what ways can I show up more as a safe haven for this partner?

....

....

....

....

....

....

Being a Secure Base for Each Other

A secure base provides the platform from which we can move out into the larger world, explore and take risks. This exploration facilitates our sense of personal competence and healthy autonomy. Being and having a secure base in our partnerships means supporting each other's personal growth and exploration, independent activities and other relationships, even when these pursuits require time apart from each other. Secure base partners will not only support our explorations, but will also offer guidance when solicited and lovingly call us on our shit.

Here are some examples of things that you and your partners can do to be secure bases for each other:

- Encourage each other's personal growth and development.
- Support each other's work and interests.
- Listen to each other's hopes, dreams and visions.
- Listen when your partners share about their experiences in other relationships (assuming that the information shared is appropriate and consensual).
- Have conversations about things that are intellectually or emotionally stimulating to each other.
- Acknowledge each other's capabilities and possibilities for growth.
- Compassionately bring light to your partner's limitations and blind spots.
- Offer words of encouragement when your partners take on new responsibilities, go on dates with others, take a risk or learn something new.

EXERCISE 7.4

For each of your relationships that are attachment-based, or for the relationships that you would like to see become more attachment-based, ask yourself:

How is this partner already acting as a secure base for me?

What does growth look like for me? Is it usually a shared experience, a personal experience or both?

Are there other ways that I want encouragement or support in my individual growth or with my visions and dreams?

How could my partners support me in regard to my other relationships?

How could I better support or encourage my partners' dreams or
aspirations to grow and develop?

How could I better show genuine interest or curiosity in things that
are important to my partners?

How could I better support my partners in their other relationships?

A few additional questions:

Do you find that your past relationships tended to be more safe havens, secure bases, a balance of the two, or neither?

Do you find yourself preferring or being more comfortable with being a safe haven, a secure base, a balance of the two, or neither?

CHAPTER EIGHT
THE HEARTS OF BEING POLYSECURE

In this chapter we focus on some more specific things you can do to cultivate being polysecure through the acronym HEARTS, which I use to encapsulate the different ingredients, skills, capacities and ways of being required for secure functioning in multiple attachment-based partnerships.

The first five letters in HEARTS cover the relational level of being polysecure. The S in HEARTS focuses on the individual level of being polysecure—more on that in Chapter Nine. An important caveat is that you do not need to be perfect in all of these things all of the time, but my hope is that if you prioritize these things at the heart of your relationships, you will discover beautiful and powerful ways to thrive in love.

H: Are You Here with Me?

The optimal functioning of the attachment system and the formation of attachment security are best facilitated by consistent interactions with significant others who are responsive to our needs for proximity. We need to know that our attachment figures are available to us, that they are within arm's reach (literally and virtually) and that they will be available and responsive when we call for them. When we experience our partners as being *here with us*, it results in the positive beliefs that our partners care about us, we matter to them and we are worthy of their love and attention. Conversely, when our partners are unavailable, unresponsive or mentally elsewhere, attachment insecurity can arise, feeding the fears and doubts that we are not valued, loved or worthy.

An important aspect to being here with our partners is the quality of our presence. Being in the same physical space does not necessarily mean that you are present with the people you're near. When you're with your partners, are you really focusing on them and giving your full attention, or are you distracted by your phone, by the stresses from the day, by your worries about the future or by your other partners? Are you really listening to your partners when they talk, or are you thinking about other things, only partially listening or mentally preparing for what you want to say next? Attachment is an embodied experience. It is first through being present with ourselves in our own bodies and present with our loved ones that we can develop and express the rest of the attachment-based skills and capacities of the HEART of being polysecure. Being present is not just putting your phone down for a few minutes. It is a way of being, from interaction to interaction, where you consciously inhabit your own body and show up with the best of your attention, offering your presence as a gift.

EXERCISE 8.1

Here are some reflection questions about being present.

How do you know when someone is being present with you? What behavior from others lets you know that they are being present with you?

....

....

....

....

....

....

How do you feel when someone is distracted or partially present with you?

....

....

....

....

....

....

....

What gets in the way of you being more present with the people you're with?

....

....

....

....

....

....

....

E: Expressed Delight

The next thing that you can do to nurture more polysecurity with your partners is to offer *expressed delight*, which means conveying your joy about who your partner is—their very beingness—versus only what they do for you or how they meet your needs. When our partners are able to articulate the ways that we are special and valuable to them, our interpersonal self-worth is supported. When we express the ways that we appreciate and are grateful for our partners, we create a culture of positivity in our relationships that allows mutual vulnerability, authenticity and joy to flourish. We can express the delight we feel for our partners through our words, our actions and our touch, as well as just the look in our eyes.

EXERCISE 8.2

Here are some reflection questions about how we express delight and receive expressed delight.

How do you know that someone is expressing delight in you (i.e., their words, actions, the look in their eyes, the quality of their touch)?

....

....

....

....

....

....

How do you best register or receive expressed delight from others?

How do you tend to offer expressed delight to others?

Does anything get in the way of you either giving or receiving expressed delight?

A: Attunement

Our attachment bonds are emotional bonds, and being able to emotionally tune into and connect with our partners is at the core of feeling safe and secure together. Attunement is a state of resonance with our partners and the act of turning towards them in an attempt to understand the fullness of their perspective and experience. Attuning to a partner does not mean that you have to agree with them and take on their experience as your own, but it does mean that you are willing to join them in their internal emotional world and their inner state of mind in order to empathize with what they are going through. Attunement is meeting your partner with curiosity and wanting to understand their feelings and needs. It is the feeling of being seen, understood and "gotten" by the other.

EXERCISE 8.3

Here are some reflection questions about attunement.

How do you know that someone is attuning to you (i.e., their words, actions, the look in their eyes, the quality of their touch)?

....

....

....

....

....

How do you most register or receive emotional attunement from others?

_____

_____

_____

_____

_____

How do you tend to attune to others?

_____

_____

_____

_____

_____

What gets in the way of you either attuning to others or being attuned to by others?

_____

_____

_____

_____

_____

R: Rituals and Routines

Our attachment system is comforted by routine and regularity. In our relationships with our attachment figures, we tend to prefer partners who are more reliable and situations where we can experience the ease of generally knowing what to expect and not be surprised to the point of disruption. The mundane rituals of everyday life can put many of our worries to rest and remind us that we are an integral part of our partners' lives, and the profound rituals of commitment ceremonies and rites of passage can significantly deepen and strengthen our bonds. The outer commitment we make to a relationship through ceremonies or officially asking someone to be our partner can offer structure and definition. The day-to-day ways that we engage with one another—the micro-routines and rituals of a relationship that we create—can be seen as the inner commitment we make to show up for the relationship wholeheartedly and not just because there might be an outer, more explicit commitment to rely on.

EXERCISE 8.4

Here are some reflection questions about rituals and routines.

What rituals and routines have been important for your sense of safety and security in relationships?

....

....

....

....

....

How do you like to be celebrated or to celebrate others?

What do you and your partners each need in order to reconnect with each other after being apart?

What things get in the way of having rituals and routines in your relationships?

T: Turning Towards After Conflict

In any relationship, ruptures are inevitable. Relationships are not static but are an ongoing flow of harmony to disharmony, rupture and repair, connection, disconnection and back into connection again. We are all different from each other and so we are all eventually going to slip up, make mistakes, say things that we wish we could take back or forget things that are important to our partners. What matters is not that we have ruptures, but how we repair them. Conflicts left unrepaired can leave lasting effects on our sense of trust, safety and security. When there is conflict and disagreement or when attunement and connection have been lost, it is how we repair and find our way back to our partners that builds secure attachment and relational resilience.

EXERCISE 8.5

Here are some reflection questions about how you and your partners turn toward each other.

Are there certain themes to the conflicts that you have with your partners?

....

....

....

....

....

When there has been a conflict or fight with someone, how do you tend to react (i.e., defensive, reactive, withdrawing, mean, overly apologetic, freezing up)?

....

....

....

....

What are some of your strengths when there has been a conflict?

....

....

....

....

....

How are you at offering a repair? What comes easily to you and what feels difficult?

....

....

....

....

....

How are you with receiving a repair from your partners?

....

....

....

....

....

EXERCISE 8.6

This HEART chart is for you and your partners to go through together. You will each acknowledge the ways that you already meet and express the different components of HEART for each other and you will also explore and specify how you would like each letter of HEART to be more expressed in your relationship. The chart is provided several times over so that you can use one per partner.

Letter	How do you already express this letter towards your partner?	How can you better express this letter with your partner?	How does your partner already express this letter to you?	How can your partner better express this letter to you?	What are one or two different behaviors that you can try out to better give this letter to your partner?
H: Here	How do you show that you are here with your partner?	How can you be more present, available or responsive with your partner?	How does your partner demonstrate that they are present with you?	What could your partner do that would enhance your sense that they are here with you?	1._____ _____ _____ 2._____ _____ _____
E: Expressed delight	How do you already show expressed delight for your partner?	In what ways can you express more delight in your partner?	How does your partner let you know that you are unique, precious and special to them?	In what different or additional ways would you like to experience expressed delight from your partner?	1._____ _____ _____ 2._____ _____ _____
A: Attunement	How do you already attune to your partner?	How could you better or differently attune to your partner?	How do you already experience your partner's attunement and feeling like they "get" you?	In what ways would you like your partner to better or differently attune to you?	1._____ _____ _____ 2._____ _____ _____

	How do you already	How could you better	How does your partner	How could your partner	
R: Rituals and routines	How do you already initiate or participate in rituals and routines in your relationship?	How could you better create, initiate or participate in rituals and routines in your relationship?	How does your partner already initiate or participate in rituals and routines in your relationship?	How could your partner better create, initiate or participate in rituals and routines in your relationship? What, if any, relationship rites of passage or ceremonies could further deepen your bond with your partner?	1. _____ _____ _____ 2. _____ _____ _____
T: Turning towards after conflict	When there has been a conflict or relationship rupture, how do you already repair well?	When there has been a conflict or relationship rupture, how can you better initiate and receive repairs?	When there has been a conflict or relationship rupture, how does your partner already repair well?	When there has been a conflict or relationship rupture, how can your partner better initiate or receive repairs?	1. _____ _____ _____ 2. _____ _____ _____

Letter	How do you already express this letter towards your partner?	How can you better express this letter with your partner?	How does your partner already express this letter to you?	How can your partner better express this letter to you?	What are one or two different behaviors that you can try out to better give this letter to your partner?
H: Here	How do you show that you are here with your partner?	How can you be more present, available or responsive with your partner?	How does your partner demonstrate that they are present with you?	What could your partner do that would enhance your sense that they are here with you?	1._____ _____ _____ 2._____ _____ _____
E: Expressed delight	How do you already show expressed delight for your partner?	In what ways can you express more delight in your partner?	How does your partner let you know that you are unique, precious and special to them?	In what different or additional ways would you like to experience expressed delight from your partner?	1._____ _____ _____ 2._____ _____ _____
A: Attunement	How do you already attune to your partner?	How could you better or differently attune to your partner?	How do you already experience your partner's attunement and feeling like they "get" you?	In what ways would you like your partner to better or differently attune to you?	1._____ _____ _____ 2._____ _____ _____

R: Rituals and routines	How do you already initiate or participate in rituals and routines in your relationship?	How could you better create, initiate or participate in rituals and routines in your relationship?	How does your partner already initiate or participate in rituals and routines in your relationship?	How could your partner better create, initiate or participate in rituals and routines in your relationship? What, if any, relationship rites of passage or ceremonies could further deepen your bond with your partner?	1. _____ _____ 2. _____ _____
T: Turning towards after conflict	When there has been a conflict or relationship rupture, how do you already repair well?	When there has been a conflict or relationship rupture, how can you better initiate and receive repairs?	When there has been a conflict or relationship rupture, how does your partner already repair well?	When there has been a conflict or relationship rupture, how can your partner better initiate or receive repairs?	1. _____ _____ 2. _____ _____

Letter	How do you already express this letter towards your partner?	How can you better express this letter with your partner?	How does your partner already express this letter to you?	How can your partner better express this letter to you?	What are one or two different behaviors that you can try out to better give this letter to your partner?
H: Here	How do you show that you are here with your partner?	How can you be more present, available or responsive with your partner?	How does your partner demonstrate that they are present with you?	What could your partner do that would enhance your sense that they are here with you?	1._____ _____ _____ _____ 2._____ _____ _____
E: Expressed delight	How do you already show expressed delight for your partner?	In what ways can you express more delight in your partner?	How does your partner let you know that you are unique, precious and special to them?	In what different or additional ways would you like to experience expressed delight from your partner?	1._____ _____ _____ _____ 2._____ _____ _____
A: Attunement	How do you already attune to your partner?	How could you better or differently attune to your partner?	How do you already experience your partner's attunement and feeling like they "get" you?	In what ways would you like your partner to better or differently attune to you?	1._____ _____ _____ _____ 2._____ _____ _____

R: Rituals and routines	How do you already initiate or participate in rituals and routines in your relationship?	How could you better create, initiate or participate in rituals and routines in your relationship?	How does your partner already initiate or participate in rituals and routines in your relationship?	How could your partner better create, initiate or participate in rituals and routines in your relationship? What, if any, relationship rites of passage or ceremonies could further deepen your bond with your partner?
				1. _____ _____ 2. _____ _____
T: Turning towards after conflict	When there has been a conflict or relationship rupture, how do you already repair well?	When there has been a conflict or relationship rupture, how can you better initiate and receive repairs?	When there has been a conflict or relationship rupture, how does your partner already repair well?	When there has been a conflict or relationship rupture, how can your partner better initiate or receive repairs?
				1. _____ _____ 2. _____ _____

Letter	How do you already express this letter towards your partner?	How can you better express this letter with your partner?	How does your partner already express this letter to you?	How can your partner better express this letter to you?	What are one or two different behaviors that you can try out to better give this letter to your partner?
H: Here	How do you show that you are here with your partner?	How can you be more present, available or responsive with your partner?	How does your partner demonstrate that they are present with you?	What could your partner do that would enhance your sense that they are here with you?	1. _____ _____ _____ 2. _____ _____
E: Expressed delight	How do you already show expressed delight for your partner?	In what ways can you express more delight in your partner?	How does your partner let you know that you are unique, precious and special to them?	In what different or additional ways would you like to experience expressed delight from your partner?	1. _____ _____ _____ 2. _____ _____
A: Attunement	How do you already attune to your partner?	How could you better or differently attune to your partner?	How do you already experience your partner's attunement and feeling like they "get" you?	In what ways would you like your partner to better or differently attune to you?	1. _____ _____ _____ 2. _____ _____

	How do you already initiate or participate in rituals and routines in your relationship?	How could you better create, initiate or participate in rituals and routines in your relationship?	How does your partner already initiate or participate in rituals and routines in your relationship?	How could your partner better create, initiate or participate in rituals and routines in your relationship? What, if any, relationship rites of passage or ceremonies could further deepen your bond with your partner?
R: Rituals and routines				1. _____ _____ _____ 2. _____ _____ _____
T: Turning towards after conflict	When there has been a conflict or relationship rupture, how do you already repair well?	When there has been a conflict or relationship rupture, how can you better initiate and receive repairs?	When there has been a conflict or relationship rupture, how does your partner already repair well?	When there has been a conflict or relationship rupture, how can your partner better initiate or receive repairs? 1. _____ _____ _____ 2. _____ _____

Letter	How do you already express this letter towards your partner?	How can you better express this letter with your partner?	How does your partner already express this letter to you?	How can your partner better express this letter to you?	What are one or two different behaviors that you can try out to better give this letter to your partner?
H: Here	How do you show that you are here with your partner?	How can you be more present, available or responsive with your partner?	How does your partner demonstrate that they are present with you?	What could your partner do that would enhance your sense that they are here with you?	1. _____ _____ _____ 2. _____ _____ _____
E: Expressed delight	How do you already show expressed delight for your partner?	In what ways can you express more delight in your partner?	How does your partner let you know that you are unique, precious and special to them?	In what different or additional ways would you like to experience expressed delight from your partner?	1. _____ _____ _____ 2. _____ _____ _____
A: Attunement	How do you already attune to your partner?	How could you better or differently attune to your partner?	How do you already experience your partner's attunement and feeling like they "get" you?	In what ways would you like your partner to better or differently attune to you?	1. _____ _____ _____ 2. _____ _____ _____

	How do you already initiate or participate in rituals and routines in your relationship?	How could you better create, initiate or participate in rituals and routines in your relationship?	How does your partner already initiate or participate in rituals and routines in your relationship?	How could your partner better create, initiate or participate in rituals and routines in your relationship? What, if any, relationship rites of passage or ceremonies could further deepen your bond with your partner?
R: Rituals and routines				1. _____ _____ _____ 2. _____ _____ _____
T: Turning towards after conflict	When there has been a conflict or relationship rupture, how do you already repair well?	When there has been a conflict or relationship rupture, how can you better initiate and receive repairs?	When there has been a conflict or relationship rupture, how does your partner already repair well?	When there has been a conflict or relationship rupture, how can your partner better initiate or receive repairs? 1. _____ _____ _____ 2. _____ _____ _____

CHAPTER NINE

THE S IN HEARTS — SECURE ATTACHMENT WITH SELF

When we have experienced attachment insecurity with attachment figures—whether in childhood, in our adult relationships or as disruptions in any of the levels discussed in the nested model of attachment and trauma—our primary relationship with our self can become severed and the development of certain capacities and skills can become compromised. Attachment ruptures and trauma can also leave lasting marks on our psyche, distorting our sense of self through the beliefs that we don't matter, or that we are flawed, broken, unworthy, too much or not enough. This is what needs to be repaired. In many ways, it's the only aspect of our healing that we are truly in control of, since the HEART of being polysecure requires partners to practice with and the other levels of the nested model require group-based or collective processes that typically go beyond the individual level.

Internal attachment healing is needed for secure functioning to become possible and then take root in our relationships. When we are relating from attachment insecurity, we can easily put too much onto our partners. We can make our partners into the source of our hope, love, strength and ability to feel or regulate our own emotions, as well as the source of our meaning and purpose in life. Our partners can be the inspiration for these things, as well as the objects or focus of our love, but they should not be the source of it. *You* are the source of your happiness, love, courage, emotional regulation and purpose. Knowing how to stand securely on your own two feet and how to be your own safe haven and secure base are fundamental to building your internal secure attachment.

EXERCISE 9.1

I call this one "Go HEART Yourself!" The HEART of secure functioning is not just for your relationships with partners, but can be directly applied to your relationship with yourself. Here are some questions for you to consider for each letter of HEART.

H: Being Here with Yourself

In general, how comfortable or uncomfortable do you feel being alone with yourself?

....

....

....

....

....

What are the subtle and overt ways that you avoid being present with yourself?

....

....

....

....

What does being present with yourself mean to you?

....

....

....

....

....

Do you have ways of centering and grounding yourself? What are they?

_____

_____

_____

_____

_____

Who do you know who seems to do this well? How do they manage this?

_____

_____

_____

_____

_____

What does being more embodied mean to you? How would that look?

_____

_____

_____

_____

_____

E: Expressed Delight for Yourself

What does expressed delight look like for you right now?

....
....
....
....
....

Do you struggle with critical and shameful inner parts that sabotage your ability to value and appreciate yourself? If so, give a name to these parts and dialogue with them about what they need.

....
....
....
....
....

What experiences would become more possible for you, in regard to yourself and your relationships, if expressed delight was more central to your inner experience?

....
....
....
....
....

If you were a close friend talking to yourself, what would you say?

A: Attuning to Yourself

What does self-attunement mean to you?

Do you tend to notice the early warning signs that you may be getting stressed, tired, hungry or emotionally triggered? Or do these experiences seem to come out of nowhere? Make a list of some early warning signs that you are off your axis and then some ideas of early interventions to help you regain your center.

Table 9.1 provides definitions of some terms that will be helpful for answering the next few questions.

Types of Regulation	
Auto-Regulation (It just happens)	• Self-stimulation or self-soothing done more automatically than consciously. • Autoregulation is done alone, so there is no interpersonal stress. • Can be similar to overfocusing on an object or task and can be dissociative or zoning out. Examples: Thumb-sucking, averting eye contact, reading, doing art, watching TV, alcohol, drugs, masturbating, daydreaming, overeating, swiping or scrolling on your phone.
External Regulation (You do it)	• Reaching for another to help regulate and soothe you. • Interactive, but only focusing on one person attuning to the other at a time. • Can overfocus on either the self or on the other. Examples: Being held and soothed by a caregiver, talking with a friend about your problems, listening to a live talk or music, getting a massage.
Interactive Regulation (We do it)	• Mutual or co-regulation with another where both people are regulating each other. • Skin-to-skin and eye-to-eye contact. • Both people are attuning to each other. Examples: Dancing with a partner, sex, having a mutual dialogue, musicians playing together, cooking together.
Self-Regulation (I do it)	• Regulating one's own state through active or intentional techniques that are self-soothing or stimulating. • Ability to exhibit self-control through managing bodily or emotional impulses. Examples: Calming down through breath control, mental techniques (e.g., reframing), muscle relaxation, vocal control. Some of the autoregulation behaviors can also be examples of *self-regulation* when they are intentional.

TABLE 9.1: Types of regulation

In what ways do you autoregulate or try to use others to regulate? How has this impacted you or your relationships?

In what ways are you able to do interactive regulation? And how can you do more interactive regulation?

In what ways are you able to intentionally self-regulate? And how would you like to increase your self-regulation?

What is your relationship with your inner nurturer like? How can this part of you become more front and center in your relationship with yourself?

R: Rituals and Routines for a Secure Self

What routines and rituals do you have that support you in your well-being and self-care?

....
....
....
....
....

Reflect on times in your past when you felt like you were in a good rhythm with yourself. What factors supported this?

....
....
....
....
....

What routines and rituals do you need to add into your day or week that would even better support you in your well-being and self-care?

....
....
....
....
....

What larger rituals or rites of passage would you like to experience?

....

....

....

....

....

What practices do you already do that align you with your better or more secure self?

....

....

....

....

....

What practices could you take on to align yourself with the secure you?

....

....

....

....

....

....

T: Turning Toward Yourself after Inner Conflict or Triggers

How do you treat yourself when you make a mistake or fall short of
your own standards and expectations?

How do you respond to yourself when you have an inner conflict?
How would you like to treat yourself differently?

What would become possible for you if you did this?

How frequently are you getting emotionally reactive and how does
this impact you?

EXERCISE 9.2

In this HEART action chart, you will focus on how you already embody each letter of HEART and what else you can do to bring it more fully into your secure relationship with yourself.

Letter	How do you already express this letter towards yourself?	How would you like to better express this letter with yourself?	What two or three behaviors or commitments can you make to this letter?
H: Being here with yourself	How do you already embody being present with yourself?	How can you be more present, available or responsive to your feelings, needs and wants?	
E: Expressed delight for yourself	How do you already show expressed delight for yourself?	In what ways can you express more delight in yourself?	
A: Attuning to yourself	How do you already attune to yourself?	How could you attune to yourself better or differently?	In what ways can you self-regulate better or differently?

Letter	How do you already express this letter towards yourself?	How would you like to better express this letter with yourself?	What two or three behaviors or commitments can you make to this letter?
R: Rituals and routines for a secure self	How do you already initiate or participate in rituals and routines that support self-care and your physical, emotional and mental health?	How could you better create, initiate or participate in rituals and routines for your self-care and your physical, emotional and mental health?	
T: Turning toward yourself after inner conflict or triggers	When there has been an inner conflict or you are triggered, what do you already do that supports you with inner repair?	What could you do to better manage your triggers,* both preventively and during an actual trigger experience?	

* Go to www.jessicafern.com for a free webinar on Rewiring Your Triggers.

EXERCISE 9.3

Based on the exercises from this section, create an image in your mind of what the *secure you* looks, feels and acts like. If you were already healed from your attachment past and embodying the different aspects of HEART, imagine what it would be like to move through your day and relate to others. Take three to five minutes to really envision what this would be like and to truly enjoy and feel it as if it were true. If you prefer to draw this out or dance and move this visualization through your body, go for it!

Earned Secure Attachment

Those of us who did not experience a securely attached childhood or who have had significant attachment insecurity from our adult relationships can still develop *earned secure attachment*. Meaningful contact with teachers, friends, lovers, mentors, therapists, spiritual guides or relatives who can empathically resonate and securely bond with us can all assist us in adjusting our attachment style towards becoming more secure. Forging an accepting and loving relationship with yourself is also key to this process. All of the exercises in this workbook aim to support your earned secure attachment. The following questions provide pathways for a continuation of the process of attaining more earned secure attachment with yourself.

Creating Your Childhood Attachment Story

At the self level, one way to develop earned secure attachment is through making sense of your story. One piece of your earned secure attachment is being able to acknowledge both positive and negative aspects of your formative family experiences and relate how these experiences impacted who you became. Chapter One covers many aspects of your history with your attachment figures and how that history shaped who you became. Thankfully, through the process of self-reflection and gaining understanding, we can free ourselves from the limitations of our upbringing. Making sense of our lives by writing a coherent narrative allows us to have a sense of who we've been, who we are now and who we'd like to become.

EXERCISE 9.4

In this exercise, you'll be writing your short childhood attachment story. It may be helpful to review your Chapter One responses, since many of the questions you answered there cover aspects of your childhood attachment narrative. I'm suggesting that you now write a short narrative that should be at least one to two pages in length, but it can be as long as you need it to be (just grab some looseleaf pages or a notebook, or use a computer if you prefer). The coherence of this narrative is what's important; the story you tell just needs to make sense to you or anyone that you would tell it to. This is not about getting into all the details of everything you went through, but more about your general experiences and your understanding about how those experiences impacted you.

Introduction section: What you were born into?

Write an opening paragraph about the general world that you were born into, meaning the time, location and cultural, social and environmental factors that had an influence on your attachment experiences. What belief systems and worldviews were you born into?

Then write more specifically about what your parents were like and briefly how the factors of their life (either what you concretely know about them or what you can assume about them) set them up to parent or not parent in certain ways.

The body of the story: What were your past attachment experiences?

Take a few paragraphs to write about your more difficult childhood attachment experiences. First, write about the significant attachment ruptures you experienced through losses, deaths, big life transitions, forms of abuse and neglect, or attachment figures being unpredictable, unavailable, misattuned, scary, too strict, aggressive, too permissive, checked out, smothering, emotionally distant or cold, and so on.

Then take a paragraph to talk about your positive attachment experiences. What experiences in your life supported a more secure attachment for you? What people or communities supported you in feeling seen, safe, special and cared for?

How did all of these attachment experiences impact you? How did they shape how you came to see yourself and what you believed about yourself? How did these experiences shape how you saw others regarding whether people were safe, trustworthy, dependable and so on? How did you see the world at large? What attachment styles did you develop because of these experiences?

Conclusion section: How are you moving forward?

Based on where you've come from, describe where you are now in your life. In what ways have your attachment styles changed or stayed the same? Give voice to the inner work and healing that you've done and end this story with where you are headed in terms of having a more secure attachment with yourself and others.

_____

_____

_____

_____

_____

_____

_____

_____

_____

_____

_____

_____

_____

_____

_____

_____

Creating Your Adult Attachment Narrative

Many of our attachment wounds are not just from our childhood, but are experienced through our adult romantic and non-romantic relationships too. In addition to any wounds we've experienced in adult attachment relationships before becoming nonmonogamous, as the book *Polysecure* explains, the process of transitioning from the paradigm of monogamy to that of nonmonogamy can also create new and additional attachment ruptures in our lives. Creating a coherent narrative of your attachment struggles and ruptures within a specific relationship or in terms of your nonmonogamous journey can support you in further mending and integrating your attachment experiences and cultivating a more earned secure attachment with yourself and with your adult attachment relationships.

EXERCISE 9.5

Here, you'll be writing a new narrative for an adult attachment relationship. Approach this in the same way you did for the childhood one in Exercise 9.4. This exercise can be done for as many relationships as you would like, whether monogamous or nonmonogamous.

Introduction: Setting the stage

What was the context that preceded the relationship you are writing about or your transition into nonmonogamy? What were the larger events, phases or influences in your life at the beginning of this specific relationship or at the beginning of your CNM journey? What led you to make the decision to enter this relationship or CNM?

The body of your story

Once you were in this relationship or beginning to practice CNM, what were your initial experiences like? Was there a honeymoon phase? Was it difficult from the start? What attachment styles were you relating from? How did you feel about yourself and the people with whom you were in a relationship?

As time passed, what changed? What became better or more challenging? Describe some of the attachment challenges or ruptures that you experienced and how they impacted you. Describe the ups and downs of your relationship or your CNM experiences.

Conclusion section: Moving forward

Where have your experiences brought you now? What choices have you made regarding your relationships or CNM? What important lessons have you learned about yourself, others and your attachment? Where are you headed and what are you committed to in terms of showing up in more empowered and polysecure ways?

....

....

....

....

....

....

....

....

....

....

....

....

....

....

....

....

CHAPTER TEN

COMMON QUESTIONS AND FINAL THOUGHTS

Polysaturation and Vessels

In the final chapter of *Polysecure* I covered two frequently asked questions: "How many attachment-based relationships can I have?" and "Should we close our relationship when there are attachment problems?" In this chapter, I'll guide you through assessing how *poly-saturated* or life-saturated you are so that you can answer the first question for yourself. Then I will guide you through some options for creating a temporary relationship container or a vessel to support you through working through attachment challenges when practicing CNM. A vessel is meant to be a short-term relationship structure that allows you to engage in certain aspects of CNM while postponing others, so that partners can better ease into the nonmonogamous relationship structure and address their attachment needs.

How Saturated Are You?

Many factors will impact the number of partners with whom you can fully enter into a secure attachment-based relationship. Using the nested model of attachment and trauma, explore how each different level might impact your ability to be more or less present and available in your relationships. In the fillable nested model under Exercise 10.1, you can list the different life factors that affect your degree of saturation within each of its levels. These are just some of the factors that can impact how much emotional bandwidth a person has for secure relationships. It's not just about how polysaturated you are, but how life-saturated you are.

EXERCISE 10.1

For each different level of the nested model of attachment, fill in the different factors that either support or lessen your ability to be available and present for yourself and for others. Use the following questions as prompts for you to come up with the possible life factors impacting your level of availability. Feel free to add any additional factors that impact you but are not named here.

Self
- How is your physical and mental health?
- Do you have an illness or any medical challenges?
- Are you experiencing a transition in how you identify your sexuality, your gender or any other aspect of yourself?
- Where are you in your healing process regarding trauma and attachment insecurity?
- Are there certain hobbies or passions that are very important for you to pursue or make time for?
- Are you in a major life transition (e.g., divorce, moving, career change, gender transition, empty nest or leaving an organized religion)?

Relationships
- How many partners do you already have and how much time and attention do these relationships take up?
- Do you have kids? If so, how many and how old are they? How much time and attention do these relationships take up?
- Do you care for elderly parents or other adults? How much time and attention do these relationships take up?
- Do you have significant non-romantic relationships and friend-ships that are important to you? How much time and attention do these relationships take up?
- Do any of your partners have specific physical, emotional or health-related needs—whether temporary or ongoing—or are they in a life transition that requires more support?

Home
- How stable or unstable is your home environment?

- Do you have a home or live on property that takes up time to manage and maintain?
- How many people do you live with? How much time and attention do these relationships take up?
- Does your home allow for privacy for yourself and with partners, and how does that impact your level of availability?

Local Communities and Culture

This level refers to the places we spend our time outside of our home or in virtual space.

- How demanding of your time and attention is your work?
- Are you in school? If so, how much time and attention does your schooling take up?
- Do you have community commitments or events that matter to you? If so, how much time and attention do these commitments take up?
- Have you lost community support because you are practicing nonmonogamy?
- Can you be out about being nonmonogamous in the different communities that you are a part of?

Social

- Do you experience oppression based on your race, class, sex, gender, ability, sexual orientation, relationship orientation or other aspects of your identity? How does this impact your life, your stress levels, your sense of safety or your ability to be present with others?
- Are there political factors that are impacting your life? If so, how do these factors impact your daily life and your levels of saturation?
- How is your level of saturation impacted by your access or lack of access to healthcare, certain legal or institutional rights or social support systems?

Global or Collective

- Do you have access to being in nature, clean water, air and soil?
- Are you experiencing the impact of global climate change or natural disasters?

- How has the COVID-19 pandemic impacted you, your life and relationships?
- How does the global economy impact your finances?

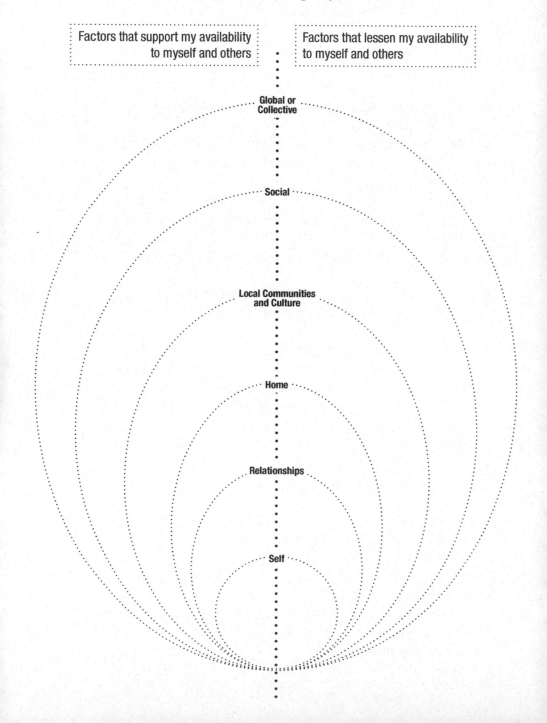

EXERCISE 10.2

Here are some overall questions to consider about polysaturation and life saturation.

When you think of your life now, which of the above factors are playing a role in how available or unavailable you are for your attachment-based relationships?

....

....

....

....

....

....

If you are in a relationship or have been in a relationship with someone who is less available than you would like, what situational factors in their life might have been contributing to this?

....

....

....

....

....

....

Here is a scale you can use to assess whether or not you have the availability for another attachment-based relationship.

1. I've got a lot of time and energy for another attachment-based relationship.
2. I have commitments in my life that take up time (i.e., children, work, friends, partners, hobbies) but I can carve out more time for someone without it having a negative impact on my other relationships or the things that are important to me.
3. I would like another partner, but that would mean taking valuable time away from other relationships or the things that are important to me. If I were to meet a very rare or unique person, it might be worth it to renegotiate some aspects of my life or other relationships.
4. The thought of another partnership might theoretically be nice, but I have way too much going on in my life to actually take on another relationship without it being stressful to me or detrimental to other relationships and responsibilities. Another relationship would not be wise right now.
5. The thought of another partnership is completely overwhelming. I am stressed and at or beyond capacity with the relationships and responsibilities I already have. I actually need to reduce my relationships, responsibilities or commitments in some way before the situation starts to harm me, others or things I care about.

Creating a Vessel When Experiencing Attachment Struggles

Sometimes going straight from being in a relationship that has been completely monogamous to something like non-hierarchical polyamory or relationship anarchy can be too much of a shock. It's possible to get there, but what I frequently see is that partners who pace out how they get there have more success and less avoidable pain and suffering in the process. Creating a temporary vessel can be one way to honor the time it takes to undo the monogamous hierarchy and couple privilege that you have been functioning in so that you can recreate your relationship in a new nonmonogamous structure. Similar to when we need training wheels to first ride a bike or crutches when we have had an injury, when a partner is struggling with higher levels of attachment insecurity, creating a temporary vessel can support them in taking steps forward with more safety and security so that their nervous system can catch up and integrate the new experiences. Taking steps in a relationship structure that you may not have initiated on your own, or one that is causing new attachment ruptures for you, will probably be uncomfortable and out of your comfort zone. I think it's important to know that trying out new things rarely feels completely comfortable and easy, but creating some type of temporary vessel can be a way to help you move forward without pushing you beyond what your nervous system can healthfully integrate.

It's important to note that the vessel you create needs to be specific to you and your partners. The vessels that I name here may or may not be the right fit for you and your situation. As well, vessels can be introduced at any point in your CNM journey, not just the beginning. Some things I suggest here may not be possible for you, depending on how far along you are into your CNM journey and what your extended partnership situation looks like. It is also important that no one makes agreements that they actually don't want to make or that they don't have the capacity to follow through with. Be honest and realistic about what you need and what you can offer.

Here are some examples of vessels that I've seen people try:

A staggered approach to dating: This is where one partner (usually the more reluctant partner who needs more experience and convincing that they can even do nonmonogamy) is the first one to start dating for a determined amount of time before the other partner starts to date or engage with other potential partners.

An experimental period of partial polyamory: Partners pick a period of several months during which they are engaging in certain types of sexual or dating experiences, together or separately, that are initially less triggering to each other. At the end of this period, they reassess what worked and what didn't and then what additional experiences they can now expand into. If you are going to do this, I believe that it is important to let the people you're dating know that you are either in a trial CNM period or that you are not yet fully available for a committed relationship so that expectations or hopes can be transparent and realistic.

Temporary polyfidelity: This is where all current relationships continue as they are, but are closed to any new partners.

Closing up: Taking a period of time to be exclusive with one partner, where you are no longer pursuing or relating to anyone in a romantic or sexual way—even through messaging or apps—in order to focus on what you need individually and together to heal and feel ready enough to move forward with nonmonogamy.

Taking a pause: This is similar to the closing up, but not as absolute in your disconnection from all your sexual or romantic connections and relationships. A person or partners taking a pause might continue to maintain some of their current connections by staying connected more as friends or less intense partners before resuming the more romantic or sexual dimensions of those relationships. Another version of this can be taking a break or pause from dating others for a few weeks and then resuming these connections just as they were before the pause. If you choose this option, please take the time to inform and include anyone this may impact, so that they are able to understand the choice you are making and consent to this process versus having a unilateral decision imposed on them.

I've found that partners who do well with creating a vessel and are able to later expand beyond the vessel tend to have at least two of these three supports:
- Weekly nonmonogamy check-ins together, such as the RADAR process outlined by the Multiamory podcast[†].
- Individual support from a professional to work on healing their respective attachment wounds, work through any jealousy or personal insecurities, and create more personal readiness for this process.
- Couples' coaching or therapy specifically for CNM and attachment repair.

---

† https://www.multiamory.com/radar

What I have seen that does *not* work well when trying to create a vessel is when:

- People try to create a vessel to control their partners, control the nonmonogamy process or control any potential metamours.
- When people do not actually want to do nonmonogamy at all and so no matter how many vessels you create to ease someone into the process, it's not going to work.
- Partners are not doing their individual inner work within the vessel in order to grow, heal and gain the skills and capacities they need to expand beyond the vessel they created.

EXERCISE 10.3

Use the following questions and prompts to craft a vessel with your partner. Take turns answering these questions and don't rush the process. Vessels that are the most supportive and successful are usually ones that have had a few revisions along the way.

When you read the above examples of possible vessels, which ones speak to you? Which ones don't? Why?

....
....
....
....
....
....

If you could craft your own vessel, what would it look like and how long would it last?

....
....
....
....
....
....

What do you think this would offer you and your relationship?

What needs does this potential vessel meet for you?

What are your intentions for the vessel? (State your intentions in positive language, focusing on what you want to experience, versus what you want to avoid.)

What commitments can you make during this time to focus on your own inner work?

....

....

....

....

....

....

What commitments can you make during this time to get support as partners?

....

....

....

....

....

....

After you and your partner or partners each share your preferred vessels, take the time to negotiate one that fits enough of what you all need and want and then go try it out. I suggest trying it out for a shorter period, say for a week or two, to make sure that each of you feels like you can fully consent to the vessel you've created and that no one has said yes to things they don't actually want to do or may not be able to realistically follow through with. Don't forget to schedule your check-ins! After the initial two-week trial period, make any necessary changes or updates to your vessel then agree to a longer time frame to implement it.

CONCLUSION

Congratulations, you did it! I truly commend you for the time and effort you put into yourself and your relationships through this workbook. Your willingness to complete these exercises is no small feat, and I hope you have strengthened your relationship with yourself and your attachment-based relationships—be it family of origin, your current partners or other important people in your life. I hope that you have gained a deeper understanding of your attachment history, how it shaped you and the gifts and strengths that you have acquired from these experiences, even if they were less than ideal. I hope that you have acquired a more embodied knowledge of what you feel, want and need, as well as how to more fully show up, tend to, give, receive and enact the HEART principles in your relationships.

The path to our healing, growth and evolution is usually more circuitous than linear. Functioning and relating in secure ways to ourselves and others is a lifetime process that changes as different partners and attachment figures come in and out of our lives. Even though you've reached the end of the workbook, I hope that you will continue on your secure attachment path. Feel free to return to this workbook whenever you feel the need to go deeper with your self-understanding and relational healing or if you just need a tune-up or refresher. I wish you all the best and all the love on your continued journey towards polysecurity.

GLOSSARY

Attachment
The deep emotional bond that takes place between two individuals. Our first attachments are as infants with our caregivers, and these lay the foundation for how safe and secure we feel within ourselves and with others later in life.

Attunement
The way we "tune in" to another's feelings and needs, doing our best to understand what might be going on for them and to respond in a way that is connected, resonant, sensitive and responsive to them.

Compersion
The state of happiness, joy or pleasure that comes from delighting in other people's happiness. In nonmonogamy, this term is more specifically used to refer to the positive feelings experienced when your lover is having a positive experience with one of their other lovers.

Co-regulation
Mutual interactions with another where both people support the calming and soothing of each other's nervous systems.

Consensual nonmonogamy (CNM)
The practice of having multiple sexual or romantic partners at the same time, where all people involved are aware of this relationship arrangement and consent to it. CNM can include polyamory, swinging, open marriage, open relationship, solo polyamory, relationship anarchy and other models.

Metamour
Two people who share a partner, but are not romantically or sexually involved with each other. For example, if you have a partner who also has a spouse, you and their spouse would be metamours, or if you have a boyfriend and a girlfriend who are not involved with each other, the two of them would be metamours to each other.

Mononormativity

This term was coined by Pieper and Bauer‡ to refer to the dominant assumptions in society regarding the naturalness and normalcy of monogamy, where political, popular and psychological narratives typically present monogamy as the superior, most natural or morally correct way to do relationships.

Polysaturated

The point at which the thought of another relationship leaves one feeling more exhausted than excited. This is when a polyamorous person has as many partners as they think they can handle at a given time.

Polysecure

Experiencing secure attachment with yourself and your multiple partners. The state of both being securely attached to multiple romantic partners and having enough internal security to be able to navigate the structural relationship insecurity inherent to nonmonogamy as well as the increased complexity and uncertainty that occurs when having multiple partners and metamours.

Primal attachment panic

High levels of stress, anxiety and sympathetic nervous system activation when someone is emotionally or physically separate from their attachment figure or fear that their relationship with their attachment figure is in danger or threatened.

Safe haven

An aspect of attachment-based relationships in which we perceive that our caregivers or partners care about our safety, seek to respond to our distress, help us to co-regulate and soothe and are a source of emotional and physical nurturance and comfort. They are the people we can turn toward when we are in need of solace and support.

---

‡ M. Pieper and R. Bauer, "Polyamory and Mono-normativity: Results of an Empirical Study of Non-monogamous Patterns of Intimacy." Unpublished manuscript, 2006.

Secure base

An aspect of attachment-based relationships where our caregivers or partners provide the platform from which we can securely turn away from them and move out to the larger world, explore and take risks. This exploration facilitates our sense of personal competence and healthy autonomy.

Self-regulation

Modulating or regulating one's own state through active and intentional techniques that are self-soothing or stimulating.